Workers Compensation
Section 32 Settlements
A Treasure or A Trap?

A Guide for Injured Workers
in The State of New York

Copyright © Michael T. Berns 2012
All rights reserved
ISBN: 1-470-17794-3
978-1-470-177942

TheInsider@InsideWorkersCompNY.com
www.InsideWorkersCompNY.com

Inside Workers Comp NY
P.O.B. 286353
New York NY 10128-0013

Also by Michael T. Berns:

Behind The Closed Doors

An insider's look at how things really work at the NYS Workers Compensation Board -And how to fix them.

ISBN: 1-440- 45303- 9
©2008
www.createspace.com/3358424

Commentaries on Workers Compensation

Commentaries on issues relating to the New York State Workers Compensation Board, New York State Court's ruling on the Board decisions, and the Board's administrative practices and staffing can be found at www.InsideWorkersCompNY.com

ACKNOWLEDGMENTS

During my 12 years as a Board Member/Commissioner at the New York State Workers' Compensation Board, I participated in thousands of hearing in which injured workers' claims were closed by either a Lump Sum Settlement or a §32 settlement[1].

While I was on the front line (sitting at the head of the table in the hearing room), I would not have had the knowledge as to how to proceed with these hearings, let alone had the administrative ability to get all the papers and hearings in order without the support of a substantial number of people.

Those people include the administrative staff at the New York State Workers' Compensation Board, particularly those clerks and examiners in Brooklyn, the district office out of which I worked, who processed the tens of thousands of §32 settlement agreements that came to the Board.

In addition, I would also like to thank four of my fellow commissioners who were there with me when the §32's came into law in 1997 and were in the forefront of the process by which these settlements made their way through the system. While the legal staff in Albany may have set the guidelines and been helpful in resolving certain legal issues, it is always those on the front lines who change policy into a practical system that works, even if it contradicts the policy of the legal advisers. Those four are Vice Chairman Jeffrey Sweet, Commissioner Karl Henry, Commissioner Carol McManus, and Commissioner Mona Bargnesi. Their attention to detail and willingness to put up with my barrage of questions and complaints helped me to better understand the process and, hopefully, have well-served those who appeared before me, not just injured workers and their families but the attorneys for both the claimants and carriers who were responsible for drafting these agreements.

1...The "§" is a symbol used in the place of the word "Section" when referring to a 'section' of a document or law and that will be the case throughout this book.

And a thanks to Chairman Robert Snashall who through his term of office from 1995 to 2002 gave me the leeway to attempt to establish some basic guidelines and to propose a standard agreement to help expedite the review and hearing process.

I would also like to thank Victor Pasternack, Esq., the managing partner of Pasternack, Tilker, Ziegler Walsh Stanton & Romano, the highly respected claimants' advocate, for his review and suggestions. His edits further support my recommendation that attorneys are an asset in the workers compensation system even to someone like me who has been involved in adjudicating workers compensation legal and medical issues for over a decade.

Finally, a special thank you to the thousands of injured workers who, at the hearings and since my 2008 departure from the Board, by e-mail and phone have come to me with questions which enabled me to better understand the help and guidance they needed.

I also must acknowledge the assistance of the attorneys for both sides. While we may have had our fair share (maybe more) of disagreements over the years, it was their questions and concerns that helped bring a lot of my focus on recommending possible solutions to resolve their issues and make sure that the agreements were processed quickly and hearing scheduled.

I would like to think that all of this has come together to make this book possible. And while this book may not answer every question or even acknowledge some of the issues that face claimants, it will go a long way to making the process better understood. And it will insure that those who either accept or refuse a §32 settlement will be able to look back on their decision and feel it was the correct one for them.

March 20, 2012

ଔଓଔଓଔଓଔଓ

TABLE OF CONTENTS

CRBOCRBOCRBOCRBO

"Living and dying is not the big issue. The big issue is what you're going to do with your time while you are here."

Bill T Jones, on the MacNeil/Lehrer Report in 1987

Introduction
WHY AM I WRITING THIS BOOK?

You have just been offered a settlement for your workers' compensation case or someone told you that you should take one but you do not really know what the settlement means, other than a *'big'* check from the carrier.

As a result of the thousands of settlement hearings I conducted during my 12 years as a commissioner at the New York State Workers' Compensation Board (Board) and, since my 1998 departure from the Board, the dozens of e-mails I have received, via my website[2], or phone calls asking about §32's, I realized that there were many questions I could answer, all at one time, by putting them all into one book

For example, exactly what does this mean:

What do they mean by *'close your case'*?
Can you close your case even if it has not been accepted/established by the Board, the carrier, or your employer?
How much money is a fair amount?
What happens if you have medical expenses in the future?
What can they do to you if you don't take a settlement?

These are only a few of the first questions that come to the mind of the injured workers (from now on referred to as *'claimant'*) when the word *'settlement'* comes up with regards to the claim. Sometimes, they are called Section 32's (after §32 of the New York State Workers' Compensation Law) or Waiver Agreements or Lump Sum settlements.

Basically:
In exchange for the carrier giving you a lump sum of money, you agree to close your case forever and never get any more money from them or anyone else for time lost at work or medical treatment related to the injuries in your case. The word *'injuries'* is also used to include diseases or any medical condition allegedly the result of something that happened to you *'out of and in the course of your employment'*, such as stress, asbestosis or long-term exposure to chemicals, loss of hearing, heart disease, carpal tunnel syndrome, etc.

And, while it seems simple for your attorney or the carrier or your buddy to explain this to you, it is not easy to understand.

Although §32 waiver agreements have been in effect since 1996 and about 10,000 a year are being done, no one has properly explained to claimants what these §32's are in terms of the long term impact on the injured workers and their families, the financial and medical implications, or even what is a fair deal.

I know this because, as a Commissioner/Board Member[3], I have conducted about 6,000 hearings which the claimant had to attend in order for their §32 to become final. I kept notes and still have mine on every single one of those cases, building up an extensive data base of information which helped me better understand them and allowed me to write this book with some degree of confidence that I know what I am writing about.

(A full chapter about §32 agreements can be found in my earlier book, which has details on the *"Philosophy, Policy, and Practices"* of the Board on §32's during my 12 years at the Board.[4])

When the §32's first came into existence, no one who wrote an agreement, either an attorney representing a claimant or one representing a carrier, really had any idea what to do. There was one law firm who used to submit §32 agreements which, after listing the names of the parties, case number, and date of injury, would be a quick three lines, agreements that were accepted in the early days by some of the commissioners:

> The parties agree to conclude this case with a payment to the claimant in the amount of $50,000 to be divided $42,500 to the claimant and a $7,500 attorney fee.

3...While the title 'Board Member' is the only used in the Law itself, the term 'Commissioner' is the one usually used to refer to the 11 of the 13 members of the New York State Workers Compensation Board. The other two members are referred to by their formal title: Chairman and Vice-Chairman

4..."Behind the Closed Doors - An insider's look at how things really work at the NYS Workers Compensation Board and how to fix them." Available at AMAZON or at www.createspace.com/3358424. See page 152 for Table of Contents.

The Board declined to assist in any way other than preparing a list of ten questions to be asked at the §32 hearing (See Appendix A, page 116). There were a lot of concerns about the §32's settlements. In 1997 when we first started to do them in New York City, two commissioners rejected every agreement that came before them.

As a result of the two commissioners' decision to reject every agreement, I was asked and agreed to do their hearings. Consequently, I was hearing as many as 50 settlement agreements a week or about 20% of the statewide total.[5] As the result of handling so many cases, I had within a short period of time developed a great deal of experience in §32's such that many attorneys and some fellow commissioners would come to me for advice. But as I note below, every attempt I made to share my knowledge with the workers' compensation community and to help my fellow commissioners was blocked by Board management. In 2007, the Board set up a program called WAMO (Waiver Agreement Management Office defined in Appendix D, page 123) to assist the attorneys, a program set up without any input from the commissioners who were doing all the §32's. One of the staff assigned to help in this project refused to attend hearings to see how they ran because he was too busy developing new procedures on how to run these hearings to attend any.

In 2002, the Board changed its policy of requiring claimants to appear before commissioners when settling their case with a §32 agreement; under the new policy, the approvals were being done by the commissioners by computer on the basis of paperwork submitted to the Board. But on April 22, 2004, in *the Matter of Hart v. Pageprint/Dekalb, 6 A.D.3d 947; 775 N.Y.S.2d 195,* the New York State Appellate Division, Third Department, ruled that the Board did not have the legal authority to approve the settlements without a hearing, that the Board's new policy was in violation of its own rules. For the next few months, the commissioners again started to consider all the §32 agreements in formal hearing, until the Board could get the rules changed. Then, in early 2006, the Board again changed the procedures, this time legally, to have all claimants seeking to resolve their case with a §32 agreement appear before a law judge and not a commissioner.

Although the information WAMO developed was basically a recitation of prior explanations of the law, its real purpose was to assist the Special

5...There were 12 commissioners who held hearings so my share should have been 8.66 %

Disability Fund[6] enter into waiver agreements for the benefit of the Fund. It was not designed to help injured workers and, to this day, there has been no attempt to explain in non-technical/legal terms to the injured worker what a §32 really means for them, something that will help them understand whether they should take one when offered, when they should attempt to get one, what should be included, what is a fair agreement, what the terms of the agreement will mean to them in the future, and what may happen if they do not enter into an agreement.

The Board's goal, at least for the past four or five years, has been to '*close*' as many cases as possible, whether the settlement is fair or even appropriate. So while a law judge at a hearing may attempt to help the claimant understand the true meaning of a §32, the Board frowns on discussions with the claimants as it is a practice which the Board claims '*takes too much time.*'

The law, like any other profession, be it medicine or fixing cars, has a lot of language unique to that profession and the words they use may not have the same meaning as it does to the general public, i.e., as used in workers' compensation law, a '*closed*' case is not a closed case[7]. So, this book is for injured workers who are not attorneys written by a former commissioner who himself was not an attorney and had to figure out what all the '*secret*' code words meant. When they appear in this book, they will be defined.

As helpful as the claimants' attorneys may be, many, particularly these days, do not have the time to go into detail as to all the aspects of the agreement. Based on the 10,000+ §32's I have done and the statistics I have on virtually every one of them (statistics which I have offered, unsuccessfully, to the Board), I developed a number of checklists as well as a list of appropriate language and inappropriate language.

In 2002 with the permission of Chairman Robert Snashall and against

---

6...The Special Funds Conservation Committee ("Special Funds") was organized in 1938 for the purpose of conserving assets of the special funds, created under Subdivision 8 of §15 and §25-a of the WCL of the State of New York

7...A '*closed*' case in workers compensation law means that there are no pending issues being fought over, hence the file could be closed for now. Until the advent of the §32, a case/claim could never be closed, i.e put in a file cabinet never to be opened again on any issue pertaining to that case/claim. Now with §32's, the term '*closed*' can be used for both the §32's which permanently close a case, as well as other cases which have no open issues and are temporarily closed.

the informal and unwritten recommendations of various Board
executives and the Office of the General Counsel, I started to develop, in
meetings with attorneys from both the carrier and claimant sides, a basic
agreement. Unfortunately, the Office of the General Counsel was able to
come up with a legal objection forcing my participation to end, thus
bringing this effort to a close. The Board has since then attempted to
develop some standard language but, as is always the case, it does so
without consultation with the parties for whom the draft language is
being drafted, with the result there is no standard agreement or language
available.

The comments and explanations that follow are mine and mine alone,
although many come from my conversations with attorneys from both
sides as well as discussions with my fellow commissioners, some of the
Board's legal and administrative staff, and, last but certainly not least,
the thousands of claimants whose cases I heard who had longer-than-
allowed conversations with me during the hearings so that I could better
learn what it was that they were seeking in the agreement but not always
finding. All the literature from the Board on §32's, as limited as it is,
discusses the legal implication of a §32. None of the Board's literature
discusses the emotional issues or the true financial issues and what doors
are opened and what doors are closed for the claimant who takes an
agreement or decides not to take an agreement.

To guide myself in the beginning when I first started to review these
settlements, I set up some basic guidelines for what I wanted to see in an
agreement. Management felt that this was none of anyone's business as
the agreements were between the claimant and carrier, but I
'*accidentally*' left some of these guidelines in a hearing part (the Board's
name for a court room) with the result that many of the attorneys began
to incorporate my suggestions into their agreements.

While in principle the goal of the workers' compensation system is to
help injured workers and employers, in practice in recent years it has
taken the position that it is not in existence to help an injured worker or
the employer understand what is the law, how it works, and what the
laws really mean. The Board's goal is simply to close as many cases as it
can. Claimants' attorneys, particularly these days, are under a lot of
pressure from the Board to adhere to a very specific set of procedures to
help eliminate conflicts or controversies between injured workers and
carriers. As a result of this pressure and a great deal of new and very
complex set of rules and regulations designed to speed the process but

not necessarily insure justice, claimants' attorneys do not have as much time as they would like to explain all the details of a settlement, let alone the day-to-day work they do, unseen by the claimant, to help that claimant get fair compensation and proper medical treatment. Unlike King Solomon who proposed to cut the baby in half to find the truth – who was the real mother – the Board doesn't ask what the parties think: it just cuts the baby in half just to not waste time speaking to the parties in the conflict.

Only the commissioners, and only at the time of the §32 settlement hearing, when everything was basically done in the claim, had the time to explain what a §32 meant to each claimant and to answer any of the claimant's questions. But even then, it was only a few commissioners who would take the time to explain. Others commissioners just wanted to get their cases done for the day so they could attend to personal matters. And the law judges today are under time pressure just to close cases with fairness, justice and explanations often having no place in their work load. More often than not and to the frustration of many hard-working and concerned law judges, claimants leave the hearing with a lot of unanswered questions, many of which they had before they entered into the negotiations to settle their claims.

I expect that this book will help answer those questions and many more.

◆The layout of this book

After explaining in the next two chapters what is a §32 settlement and its history in New York State Workers' Compensation Law, there follows a standard agreement I proposed many years ago. Many of the points in my generic agreement can be found in agreements currently presented to the Board, but often in a different order and occasionally three or four times the length. Each section of my generic agreement is followed by a brief commentary with reference to specific chapters that follow, chapters that go into far more detail about all aspects of an agreement: medical expenses, compensation, what is a fair deal, legal fees, and much more. While these chapters are written in an order that I felt was appropriate, each chapter stands on its own. And, while a specific chapter may answer all of your questions, the answers make more sense in the context of the entire agreement, hence in the context of the entire book.

Some of the information is repeated several times in this book but I read a lot of text books and science journals and understand what a nuisance it is to have to flip back through what I have read (or skipped) to get an answer or a definition.

◆What this book is not

<u>This is not a legal handbook. And I am not now nor have ever been an attorney or a judge.</u> New York State over the years has passed legislation allowing those without formal legal training to act as if they were judges. But this is limited to a number of agencies which deal in what is called '*administrative law*'. The Workers' Compensation Board is one such board: only four of its 13 members must be attorneys and in my 12 years on the Board, the most attorneys we ever had on the Board at one time was five. The Department of Labor also has non-attorneys who review final appeals. However, in all these agencies the administrative law judges are all members of the New York State Bar.

This discussion and samples included in this book are based on issues and questions relating to these settlements, §32's, as they are in the State of New York. Many of these explanations will hold true for any state in the United States in which injured workers can close their cases with a similar settlement. But even in this book, the formal laws passed by the New York State legislature, the rules and regulations that interpret how those laws will apply to settlements, and the Board's own practices are constantly changing.

In fact between the date I started to write this book and the date I am finishing it, there have been two major court decisions relating to §32 agreements. The New York State Court of Appeals decision of November 16, 2011, in *The Matter of Raynor v Landmark Chrysler* may impact on the value of settlements. In fact, I differ in my interpretation of the impact of this decision in that I feel that the matter is not closed where as some attorneys feel otherwise. But more on that in Chapter 6 - *What is a Good Dollar Value*, which starts on page 50. In another decision, *The Matter of Cooper v Cosmopolitan Care* decided by the New York State Appellate Court, Third Department on November 24, 2011, reemphasized that once a §32 settlement has been approved the case is closed forever.

This book is a guide but is not in and of itself the sole resource someone should use when considering a §32 settlement. And I am certain that many attorneys as well as staff at the Board will question what I have included in this book, what I have left out, and how I have interpreted the law, rules, and regulations.

The fact that I may consider myself somewhat of an expert on workers' compensation law[8] and while many may agree that I am quite knowledgeable on the subject, **I AM NOT AN ATTORNEY** and I can neither by law nor by my own choice offer legal advice. This book is designed to explain to you the many options and choices for you to think about when considering a §32 settlement to close your case. I raise questions for you to consider and, in some cases, offer possible answers. **BUT**, if you want someone to tell you '*Yes*' or '*No*' or '*not enough*' or '*too much*' when you have to make a decision about some aspect of the agreement or the entirety of the agreement, I am not that person. Your attorney is that person and, as I emphasize in Chapter 4 (see page 33), you most likely will be better served by an attorney or licensed representative[9] who specializes in workers' compensation law.

CRSOCRSOCRSOCRSO

8...My records show that I did substantially more §32 settlement hearings than any other commissioner and I was the commissioner called on by various chairmen over the years when a settlement hearing involved well-known and/or controversial public figures.

9...Hereafter, a '*licensed representative*' will be referred to as a '*licensed rep*', the term commonly used in the workers compensation community.

Chapter 1
WHAT IS A §32

A §32 is an agreement between two parties to settle a claim: the injured worker on one side and, on the other side, the carrier that has been responsible for the claim or possibly the employer[10].

The §32 basically states that the claimant, usually in exchange for a certain sum of money, agrees to waive (a $20 legal term for *'give up'*) the right:

1. To any <u>future payment of compensation</u> that may have been awarded by the Board, even if the injury gets worse or the claimant suffers from new problems as a consequence of the initial injury and the claimant can not work in the future because of it.
2. For the carrier to <u>pay for any future medical treatment</u> that may have been approved by the Board if the case were not settled by a §32.
3. To have any <u>other carrier or health plan </u>(with rare exceptions) pay for any future medical expenses that related in any way to the initial injury. See page 63 in Chapter 7 - *Medical Expenses* and see page 98 in Chapter 13 - *Medicare & Set Asides*.
4. To reopen the case which has been closed forever. It can not be reopened no matter what happens, an interpretation of the law supported by several court cases, as noted in Appendix J - *Closed means 'CLOSED'*, page 141.

◆Settlements by Status of the Claim

An offer to settle a case or claim may come at any time during a case. When §32 settlements first appeared in 1997, I used to say that if someone tripped and fell at work, before their nose hit the ground, there would be a §32 under it, to soften the impact.

1. A claim may not yet have been accepted or disallowed. The purpose of the §32 agreement is to settle the claim, often without

---

10...Sometimes it is not a carrier but a large employer approved by the State of New York to be self-insured. For the remainder of this book, self-insured employers or trusts, which are groups of self-insured employers, shall be considered as carriers unless otherwise noted.

a decision as to whether it was a compensable claim or if should have been disallowed, i.e., *"Here's some money. Go away and we don't have to decide who is at fault."*

2. A claim may have been established but disagreement over awards for compensation or medical treatment are being controverted and both sides, to eliminate the risk of *'losing'*, agree to settle and close the case.

3. The claimant has been classified[11] and there are no further disputes but either the claimant wants to close the case forever or the carrier wants to get the case off its books[12] and therefore agrees to close the case with a settlement.

4. Sometimes, but rarely, only part of the claim is settled once and for all, while other parts of the claim continue to be under the auspices of the Board. Although the Board does accept a C-300 *'stipulation'* which can resolve once and for all a specific issue being fought over, few of these are done. And they can not be used to deal with medical treatment, per NYCRR §300.5(b)(1).

The *'concept'* of the waiver deal is simple, like buying a house. . . . the devil is in the details.

I do not know where the majority of those who read this book live, but I live in New York City in a cooperative apartment and am asked to review and approve contracts of sale and all the accompanying legal and financial documents three to four times a year. The standard fill-in-the-blanks contract is 22 pages long, accompanied usually by an additional eight or more pages of amendments, another five or six pages of forms mandated by the City and State, and as often as not, both the agreement and amendment have hand written notes all over them. And I have seen dozens of law suits over the meaning of these words in the contracts and/or amendments and/or the accompanying documents. One contract for the sale of an apartment ran 700, yes, 700 pages in length. Simple in

---

11...CLASSIFICATION: A determination by a law judge to the effect that the claimant's condition is both stable and has been measured as meeting one of the classifications of disability..

12...As long as a case is 'open' the carrier must keep a certain amount of money in a 'reserve' fund in order to have sufficient money set aside to pay future expenses of the claim, including compensation and medical expenses.

concept but the devil is in the details.

Your §32 is no different .... so here goes.

CRBOCRBOCRBOCRBO

Chapter 2
SETTLEMENTS PRIOR to §32's

Until the passage of the 1996 amendment to the New York State Workers' Compensation Law (WCL), once a claimant was injured the case was always open in the sense that the claimant could always, if the claimant qualified, get free medical care and additional compensation for lost time from work due to the injury. This was true even if they changed employers or even occupations. But since the case was still open and the carrier may be paying compensation or for occasional medical treatment, the claimant was subject to investigations and questionnaires, what many injured workers felt were lifelong intrusions into their personal life by the employer, the carriers and, by extension, the State of New York.

The Court of Appeals, in *The Matter of Martin v C.A. Productions Co.*, 8 N.Y.2d 226; 168 N.E.2d 666; 203 N.Y.S.2d 845; 1960, wrote in part that

> "§32 of the Workmen's Compensation Law (prohibiting compromise and waiver) is intended to protect a claimant from his own improvidence and folly." It added, citing a former case, "in our view, since the rule of Russell v 231 Lexington Ave Corp, 266 NY 2d 391 has been recognized and followed, and has not met with the apparent disapproval of the Legislature, it does not seem appropriate to consider a reversal of the policy announced in that case.," which "prohibit[s] compromise and waiver [and] is intended to protect a claimant from his own improvidence and folly."

But on September 10, 1996, the State Legislature did decide to change §32 which prevented *'comprise and waivers'*.[13] It passed Chapter 6350 which added a subsection §32-a to §32 of the Workers' Compensation Law to allow claimants (or their dependents in a death case) in New York to do what injured workers could do in most other states: close their case forever by getting a onetime settlement in lieu of future compensation and medical expenses and get out of the workers' compensation system forever. Although the section of the law is §32-a, the term §32 is what is commonly used except in formal legal documentation.

Before this change in the law, a claimant could make a deal with one of the finance companies that offered to give the claimant an advance on

---

13...The September 10, 1996 amendment went into effect 120 days later: December 10, 1996.

future payment in exchange for the claimant signing over to the finance company the claimant's rights to those future payments. But under New York State laws, both then and now, the claimant could take the finance company's money and still get future payment because New York State's Workers' Compensation Law does not allow the claimant to sign away those future payments nor for the finance company to require the workers' compensation carrier or employer to repay it. But, if claimant did this, the finance company could sue the claimant in civil court but, even if the finance company won, they could not attach or place a lien on the claimant's compensation awards - yes on their house, car, and bank accounts, but not the payment from the workers' compensation carrier, until the money was deposited into a checking or savings account. The only entity that by law is allowed to require the carrier to pay to them and not the claimant is the State of New York and it is only for a limited number of conditions (see page 84 in Chapter 11 - *Is the Money All Yours?*). States (New York or any other), federal, or local tax authorities can not put a lien on your awards, nor can your former spouse for past due alimony, and the credit card or auto finance company can not garnish your awards, that is until you cash or deposit your check from the carrier.

The legislation itself was relatively short in length with the real-world interpretation of the law and the procedures for implementing the law to be left up to the Board.

To understand the implications of the legislation in this matter (as with all legislation passed by every legislative body in the world) which was the result of several issues being resolved between carriers, employers, and unions, I offer the following:

> Michael D. Langan, a former U.S. Treasury official wrote the following in an op-ed entitled "The Language of Diplomacy":
>
> At one point in my federal government career, I wrote up an explanation of a complicated matter in which I considered to be an extremely clear, cogent manner. The senior government official to whom I reported read it carefully, ruminating and adjusting his glasses as he read it. Then he looked up at me and said "This isn't any good. I understand it completely. Take it back and muddy it up. I want the statement to be able to be interpreted two or three ways." The resulting ambiguity enabled some compromise between competing government interests.[14]

14... From "The Stuff of Thought" by Steven Pinker 2007 published by the Penguin Group

And thus it has been left up the Board, its legal staff, the commissioners, and the law judges to attempt to interpret how the New York State Legislature wanted these agreements to be used.

The legislation itself reads:

ARTICLE 2. COMPENSATION
§32. Waiver agreements
Workers' Compensation Law covering §32 Waiver Agreements

No agreement or release except as otherwise provided in this chapter by an employee to waive his right to compensation under this chapter shall be valid.

    a. Whenever a claim has been filed, the claimant or the deceased claimant's dependents and the employer or his carrier may enter into an agreement settling upon and determining the compensation and other benefits due to the claimant or their dependents. The agreement shall not bind the parties to it, unless it is approved by the board. Such agreements, when so approved, notwithstanding any other provisions, shall be final and conclusive upon the claimant, the claimants dependents, the employer and the insurance carrier.

    b. The agreement shall be approved by the board in a decision duly filed and served unless:

    1. the board finds the proposed agreement unfair, unconscionable, or improper as a matter of law;

    2. the board finds that the proposed agreement is the result of an intentional misrepresentation of material fact; or,

    3. within ten days of submitting the agreement one of the interested parties requests that the board disapprove the agreement.

    c. A decision duly filed and served approving an agreement submitted to the board shall not be subject to review pursuant to section

twenty-three of this article.[15] However, a
decision duly filed and served disapproving an
agreement submitted to the board is subject
to review pursuant to section twenty-three of
this article. If the board disapproves of an
agreement it shall duly file and serve a notice
of decision setting aside the proposed
agreement.

    d. An agreement for compensation and other benefits
covered by this chapter may be modified at anytime by
agreement of all interested parties provided it is
approved by the board.

In addition to WLC §32, the Board also published NYCRR §300.36[16]
which is a *"Statement of Purpose"*, explaining the goal of the §32
agreement and the basic procedures set forth by the Board to administer
and approve these agreements. The entire text of WCL §300.36 can be
found in Appendix I on page 139.

◆Lump Sum Settlement - Prior to §32's

Prior to the passage of WCL §32-a, claimants who had permanent partial
disabilities (PPD) could qualify for what was called a Lump Sum
Settlement under WCL §15-5b. Now, the term *'lump sum settlement'* is
often used to refer to §32's, as the settlements originally done under WCL
§15-5b stopped being written in about 1999 or 2000.

In order to qualify for the original §15-5b lump sum settlement, the
claimant had to have been classified as a PPD and to have had no medical
treatment for their work-related injures during the prior six months. The
six months was supposedly to prove that the claimant's condition had
stabilized and reached Maximum Medical Improvement (MMI).
Settlements were usually for five years worth of payments but could be
as little as one year or 10 years depending on the specifics of each case. If
there was a need for occasional medical treatment after the lump sum

15...Appendix J - Closed Means "CLOSED", on page 141, explains that once the
settlement is approved, there is no "do over", an interpretation of the law
supported by a New York State Appellate Court decisions: see Appendix J:
Closed means Closed on page 141.

16...NYCRR - New York Codes, Rules, and Regulations is the name for a section
of the law written usually written by each state agency/board which details how
that agency conducts its day-to-day activities.

settlement was approved, if the carrier had an objection, there was the need for a new hearing but in most cases, minor treatment was approved. But virtually all the claimants who had requested that their case be reopened had their requests denied.

Of the 655 lump sum settlements which I have in my data base, the dollar ranges were:

Under $20,000	4%
$20,000 to $29,999	13%
$30,000 to $39,999	19%
$40,000 to $49,999	17%
$50,000 to $59,999	13%
$60,000 to $79,999	17%
$80,000 to $99,999	10%
Over $100,000	7%

When the Board had its own doctors, up through 1996, the claimants would be told to arrive at the Board offices at 9:00AM for a quick medical exam to confirm their PPD status after which they would, as a group, appear before a single commissioner who would read them the rules and limitations of the lump sum settlement, known as THE SPEECH. At the end of this 'reading', the claimants would then be called in one at a time, interviewed to make sure they understood what they were doing, and the commissioner would issue a decision, in most cases approving the lump sum settlement.

Because all of the claimants had to meet the same PPD requirements and not had medical treatment for at least the prior six months, it was decided by the Board to hold a hearing at which the legal concepts and responsibilities and restrictions of the claimants would be duly noted in a speech given by the Commissioner.

The purpose of the speech was to make sure that the claimants understood that once the case was closed with a lump sum settlement, while it could be reopened for both medical needs and an increase in the rate of disability, it would be very difficult to do so.

In Appendix B: _My Lump Sum Speech_ on page 117, I have included a copy of my Lump Sum speech. The speeches given by the commissioners were similar in the topics discussed but some were a page in length and a few, like mine, three pages. I think that I had one or two claimants every year, after hearings my speech, decide not to pursue the settlement. The section that got most of their attention was three paragraphs, the last three on the second page of my speech, which I added to make sure that there was no question as to what was meant by '*no more medical*'.

After the speech was done, the claimants would sit outside the hearing part and be brought back into the hearing part one at a time for the commissioner to review their agreement with them. Because all the claimants had a PPD, no recent medicals, and were receiving regular compensation awards, all the agreements used the same Board-designed form – Form C-15 – to fill in the details of the specific agreement reached with the carrier. They would be sworn in and asked a series of questions. (My questions are in Appendix C: *My lump sum hearing questions* on page 121).The reason I had written questions down on a sheet of paper was to make certain that I would not miss any important points; I also gave a copy of this to the translators we used so that they would be sure to follow my statements and questions and translate exactly what I said, rather than paraphrase it and miss something important. Over the years, I conducted hearings that were translated in nearly 50 languages and dialects.

The C–15 form that was used for these lump sum settlements also had questions which asked about marital status, spouse's income, amount of rent, number of kids, etc. although most of the commissioners did not use this information in deciding whether or not to approve the lump sum settlement.

Virtually all cases were approved, with maybe only one in 100 claimants deciding not to proceed and another five of 100 claimants asking for a few weeks to reconsider.

◆Lump Sum Legal Fees

Attorney fees usually ran 10%. Since all the claimants had been classified, we asked if there were any '*unpaid unaccrued fees*'.

Unpaid unaccrued legal fees came about because of the way legal fees are paid to the claimants' attorneys in the workers' compensation system:

> All fees, after approval by the law judge, are deducted from the bi-weekly payments to the claimant by the carrier who then periodically pays the fee to the attorney. For example, if a claimant was classified as having a PPD, the fee was often equal to 10 weeks of compensation. When fees were awarded, they often were to be paid out of future compensation at the rate of about 10% of the

weekly award. Therefore, if the claimant was getting $400 a week, the total fee could be $4000 and the amount deducted for the fee would be at the rate of $40 a week for 100 weeks. The law judge would also indicate how often the check had to be sent by the carrier to the attorney, usually in increments of $200. Therefore there were cases in which the lump sum settlement was made before the entire fee was paid: there was $160 that had been set aside from four weeks of awards but not yet sent to the attorney. When we asked if there were any unpaid accrued legal fees, we were just asking if there were any in existence, and then, as was the common practice, these accrued but unpaid fees would be waived by the claimant's attorney and that money, i.e., $160, paid to the claimant.

For reasons not clear to anyone to whom I spoke in New York City and Long Island, an extra $100 was added to the legal fee, supposedly for arranging the medical examination that took place just prior to the hearing. The fact that the exam was always at the Board offices with a doctor who was a Board employee meant that the claimant's attorney spent no time (at least not $100 worth) to arrange the medical exam, but they asked for and got the additional $100 in New York City.

However, once the §32 waiver agreements were allowed, these lump sum settlements virtually disappeared. And, by 2000, there were none being offered by the carriers.[17] For the carrier, the §32 definitively closed the case without any possibility of reopening and there would be no more claims for additional medical or higher degree of disability, and thus a higher rate of compensation, because, under the law, lump sum settlement could be reopened.

My personal records show that from the date I did my first §15(5b) lump sum settlement after joining the Workers' Compensation Board in December of 1996 until they basically phased out in 2000, I did nearly 3000 lump sum settlements, and only had about 50 come to me for reopening. Of those, only three or four were approved for reconsideration for reopening. Requests for reopening went to a panel of three commissioners but did not necessarily include the commissioner who actually approved the original lump sum settlement.

17...On occasion, a §32 agreement will be for compensation only, excluding medical, i.e. the carrier continued to be responsible for the claimant's medical expenses as if there were no §32 on the compensation awards. While in principle the same as a lump sum settlement, the policies and procedures that cover these agreements are those of the standard §32. See Chapter 8: _Agreements Which Exclude Medical_, page 70 .

But, while practically speaking, a lump sum settlement closed over 99% of the cases forever, the fact is that if a claimants want the case reopened when they need additional medical treatment, the carrier has the right to investigate the claimant. And for many claimants, this meant that there was a Damocles sword hanging over them and they just wanted to get out of the system. The carriers wanted out, too, for they had to keep funds in a special reserve until the case was really closed, which did not happen with a lump sum settlement.

The basic concept behind the §32 was for both sides to get rid of that Damocles sword once and forever.

CSEOCSEOCSEOCSEO

Chapter 3
A BASIC §32 AGREEMENT

The text that follows is a generic agreement that in 2002 I proposed should be used for §32 settlement agreements. The language was based on my review, just for that project, of over 300 agreements, which ranged from two to 15 pages.

Some of the agreements I reviewed had minimal information and others had pages of text that even some of the attorneys attending the hearing could not explain. I know, because I would often ask them what the language meant and more than once was told *"I don't know. It's just what we use."*[18]

The §32 settlement agreement, as a written document, is

V E R Y   I M P O R T A N T

for the claimant. It is the historical summary of the claim and the injury and will be used occasionally in the future when the claimant seeks medical coverage for these or other injuries, Social Security, Medicare, Medicaid, and other medical and legal issues.

As noted in Chapter 7: _Medical Expenses_, Chapter 13: _Medicare & Set Asides_, and Question2 #13 and #21 in Chapter 14: _Frequently Asked Questions_, the §32 agreement may be used by other agencies in determining the claimant's future benefits and medical treatment. A mistake in this document can delay or even stop the claimant from receiving a proper decision on future benefits. If the agreement erroneously lists the site of injury as the left leg but it was really the right leg, there is no way that Medicare or anyone else will believe that it was the right leg that was injured. And if the §32 agreement mistakenly shows the claimant's name as John Smith, John J. Smythe is going to have problems using this document in the future.

On occasion, when the claim is first entered into the Board's system, there may be a typing error in the name or social security number. And later, the sites of injury may be in error; the case may have started with a

---

18... Unfortunately much of the practice of workers compensation law (and probably unemployment law, disability law, etc) is based on what was done in the past, even if no one knows why it started out that way or has changed slightly over the years.

right hand injury and have been changed to a right arm injury but the file still shows right hand. And since all subsequent documents are computer generated, no one notices that an error has been in the file for years, as the error is automatically printed over and over again. These errors can be easily fixed at any time that the case is open and/or can be fixed in the §32 agreement. But what is in the final §32 agreement becomes the history of the case, regardless of any underlying medical records or legal documents.

[Editor's note: The generic text of the agreement in this chapter is <u>written in a different font</u> to distinguish it from the commentary on each section of the agreement. A complete copy of this generic agreement for copying or scanning can be found in Appendix E, page 129]

The Generic §32 Agreement
The Opening Paragraph

The parties, listed below, have decided to settle this claim under §32 of the Workers' Compensation Law. The claimant agrees that by participating in a §32 agreement, the claimant is waiving the right to have the Workers' Compensation Board determine, through litigation and/or the administrative hearing process, the right to continuing payments, value of the claim, and access to future medical treatment, which could result in the value of the claim and value of future medical treatment being greater than, less than, or equal to the value of this §32 agreement. The parties to this agreement are:

```
Claimant _____[1]_____
WCB #_____[2]_____
Carrier __[3]__ on behalf of the employer\ __[3]__
```

[1] It is essential that in this document the claimant's name be written correctly, including middle initials if any. And if the claimant has married since the original filing of the accident, it would be appropriate to list both the claimant's current name as well as the one used when the claim was first filed. If a social security number is included in the agreement, it should be correct.

[2] The WCB claim number is supposed to be entered in the event that the claimant has more than one claim but only one is being settled. If there is a new claim in the future, including the WCB number in this agreement makes it easier to review the files and papers and eliminates

confusion with other cases that the claimant may have.

[3] The carrier paying the settlement is listed here. Sometimes there may be more than one carrier and/or some special New York State created funds.[19] For the claimant this makes no difference. This is for the benefit of the carrier(s). The same holds true for the employer. The only time the name of the employer is important for the claimant is when it is the employer (self-insured or otherwise) who is paying for the settlement.

> This settlement agreement is the culmination of the following history. This case is established for injuries to the claimant's __
> __[4]__ as the result of an accident on ___[5]___. The average weekly wage has been established at $__[6]___. Based on the medical evidence in the file, at a hearing of ___[7]__, the Workers' Compensation Board classified the claimant as permanently partially disabled, symptomatic treatment was authorized, and carrier/Self-insured was directed to continue payments to the claimant at ___[8]___ reduced earnings.

[4] This is where the sites of injury are listed. It is ESSENTIAL that (a) all sites of injury be accurately listed, (b) sites that have been disallowed be listed, and (c) sites still being controverted (fought over) are resolved. Chapter 7: _Medical Expenses_, page 63, explains why this attention to detail is so important.

[5] In some cases, such as occupational disease, dates of accident may not yet have been formalized. It is essential that the '_date of accident_' be inserted here, accurately.

[6] In those cases in which the claimant's average weekly wage has been set, it is a good idea to include it in the agreement.

[7] If the claimant has been formally classified [20], it is a good idea to

19... These are the UEF (Uninsured Employers Fund), Special Funds, and the Second Injury Fund, all detailed in Chapter 12 - _Who Participates in the Agreement?_ See Page 92. The entity know as the State Insurance Fund is actually a carrier for workers compensation insurance managed by the State of New York and which competes with other private carriers to sell workers compensation policies to employers.

20...CLASSIFICATION: A determination by a law judge to the effect that the claimant's condition is both stable (permanent) and has been determined to meet one of the classifications of disability: mild, moderate, total, etc.

enter that date into the agreement.

[8] As someone who reviewed thousands of these agreements, it was helpful to know the weekly rate of compensation in order to determine if the settlement amount in the agreement was *'fair'* - See Chapter 6: *What is a Good Dollar Value?*, page 50.

> The carrier/Self-insured agrees to continue payments to the claimant at ___[9]___ reduced earnings up until
> - the date of the hearing at which this agreement is approved or the date it is approved via an administrative decision.
> - the date final approval is issued by the Board.
> - the date of the filing of this agreement.
> - Other date _____

[9] In the event that the claimant has not been classified (or has been classified), this wording confirms that the carrier will continue to pay or has been paying the claimant the compensation rate previously awarded by a law judge, with that payment to continue until the date listed in one of the above options. This eliminates any misunderstanding as when the carrier can stop paying the weekly awards: the date of the hearing, the date the agreement is final (10 days later), or the date the settlement check is dated and mailed.

> The carrier/Self-insured agrees to pay to the claimant the sum of $ __[10]__ , in full and final settlement of all claims of workers' compensation indemnity and medical benefits. Said amount shall be payable within ten days after the filing of the Decision approving this Agreement. The award is allocated at the $ ___[11]___ rate.

[10] This the gross amount of the settlement, before the deduction of the attorney's fee and any other liens that may exist (See Chapter 11: *Is The Money All Yours?*). Sometimes if there are no deductions other than the legal fee, some additional wording may be added: "..medical benefits, $___ Net after legal fees."

[11] Since Social Security looks at other forms of income, including workers' compensation awards, if the claimant receives an advance payment (lump sum or §32 settlement), a calculation must be made to determine what would be the weekly value of the lump sum settlement; the result is called an *'allocation rate'*. The *'allocation rate'* is inserted if there is any possibility that the claimant may be in the process of getting

Social Security or Social Security Disability or may already be collecting it. This is a weekly rate and is usually the same as the amount of the compensation award the claimant has been receiving. If the settlement does not include an *'allocation rate'*, Social Security will calculate one, usually to the disadvantage of the claimant. The reason is that Social Security and Social Security Disability payment rates may be affected by the allocation rate. The claimant's attorney can advise the claimant if this is relevant to the claimant's agreement and what financial impact, if any, it has.

WAIVE FURTHER CLAIMS FOR COMPENSATION
The claimant hereby stipulates that there is no further claim for causally related disability, lost wages or reduced earning capacity that may arise subsequent to the date of approval of this settlement and that no additional claim shall be filed against the employer and/or its workers' compensation carrier/self-insured, directly or consequentially related to the injuries covered by this claim.

Either at the time of the settlement or on occasion well after the settlement, the claimant's work-related injuries may result in an absence from work. Be the absence for a few hours, days, weeks, or permanently, this section means that the claimant can not ask or expect the carrier to pay any compensation for that lost time. How the employer for whom the claimant is working when the absence occurs deals with this absence is between the claimant and the employer.

ONGOING MEDICAL
The carrier/Self-insured agrees to audit and pay for all medical bills, subject to medical arbitration and the New York Workers' Compensation Fee Schedule, for treatment of established, causally related sites of injury rendered prior to the approval date of this agreement. Payment of all other medical bills shall not be the responsibility of the carrier/Self-insured. The carrier/Self-insured also agrees to withdraw all C-8.1 objections[21] upon approval of this settlement agreement. The claimant also stipulates that there is no further claim for additional medical treatment, transportation, or miscellaneous expenses arising from this accident. The claimant further agrees that any need for medical

---

21... The C-8.1 is a form carriers use when they object to some aspect of a bill submitted by a medical provider: type of treatment, cost of that treatment, and/or need for or frequency of treatment.

treatment which may arise subsequent to the approval of this
agreement will be the claimant's responsibility solely and not the
responsibility of the employer and/or its workers' compensation
carrier/self-insured.

The carrier agrees to be financially responsible for bills for treatment to
all causally related sites of injury, but only up to the date of the
settlement unless another date is specifically noted in the agreement.
After the settlement is final, the expenses for new treatment become the
responsibility of the claimant and/or the private heath insurance carrier.
This is why it is ESSENTIAL that (a) all sites of injury be accurately
listed, (b) sites that have been disallowed be listed, and (c) sites still
being controverted (fought over) are resolved. See page 63, Chapter 7:
Medical Expenses for details of what this section means if there is need
for future medical treatment and if some old bills for medical treatment
show up. Bills for treatment before the settlement for the work- related
condition that arrive after the settlement date are the responsibility of the
carrier.

SOCIAL SECURITY - MEDICARE OFFSET
select one

•Upon entering into this §32 agreement, it is agreed by the parties that
$__[12]_____ of the total consideration of this settlement is
allocated for the claimant's future medical expenses related to the
injuries referred to in this settlement pursuant to the Medicare as a
Secondary Payer, statute 42 CFR 411.26 and 42 CFR 411.47.

• The claimant hereby acknowledges that they are not currently
receiving nor applied for Social Security benefits in connection with the
injuries arising from this claim.

[12] As noted in Chapter 13 - *Medicare & Set Asides* page 98, Medicare
may have an interest in the settlement. The amount listed here means that
a specific amount of the settlement is considered to be for medical
expenses and the balance for lost time from work.

In settlements over a certain size, formal approval must be gotten from
Medicare who must also approve the amount of the medical set-aside[22]
which is often calculated, not by the carrier, but by private sector

---

22...A Medicare Set Aside (MSA) is a sum of money allocated from an insurance
or workers compensation settlement to prevent the shifting of responsibility for
paying medical expenses from a primary payer to the Medicare program.

companies whose main business is doing these estimates of future medical expenses related to the claim. Further information, most of which is very complex, and always changing, can be found at the Centers for Medicare and Medicaid Services at http://www.cms.gov/WorkersCompAgencyServices/

In those agreements that do not have a formal set-aside, money is included in the settlement for future medical expenses but it is lumped in together with the compensation portion rather than specifically being identified. Why is this done? Because that is the way it has always been done.

FEE

The parties agree that an attorney's fee in the amount of $__[13]__ will be deducted from the claimant's settlement as a lien and paid directly to the claimant's attorney ___Attorney name___ subject to the Workers' Compensation Board approval.

[13] The fee, which is negotiated between the claimant and the attorney, has warranted an entire chapter of its own: Chapter 9 - *§32 Legal Fees*, page 72.

SPECIAL FUNDS CONSERVATION COMMITTEE
select one

● Special Funds Conservation Committee agrees to reimburse the carrier/Self-insured $__[14]__ of the settlement, subject to a finding of liability under Workers' Compensation Law §15(8)(d) and less any statutory retention period remaining at the time the agreement is approved. This consent is not to be construed a concession under Workers' Compensation Law §15(8)(d).

● Special Funds Conservation Committee agrees to reimburse the carrier/Self-insured $__[14]__ of the settlement, pursuant to §15-8 (or could be §14-6).

● The carrier/Self-insured agrees to withdraw its C-250 application pending approval of this settlement.

[14] As noted in comment [3] above, there are various New York State funds which, on occasion, have some financial responsibility in a claim. But the participation of these funds deals with determining how much of the settlement each of the funds or carriers must contribute. It does not

affect the amount of money offered: the more funds there are does not mean more money for the claimant. One of the three paragraphs above is inserted to resolve the open issues between the carrier(s) and the fund(s). On occasion one of these funds may be the only carrier involved in the agreement and therefore would be listed in [3] at the beginning of the agreement.

THIRD PARTY SUITS - WCL §29
select one [15]

• Although the parties are unaware of any pending third party action, the carrier/Self-insured hereby reserves all rights to offsets and liens pursuant to §29, in relation to any third party action(s) brought as a result of this claim.

• All parties acknowledge that a third party action brought as a result of this claim

    • has commenced and been taken into consideration by all parties in the above noted settlement and the Carrier/Self-insured agrees that it is **retaining** all rights to offsets and liens pursuant to §29.

    • has commenced and been taken into consideration by all parties in the above noted settlement and the Carrier/Self-insured agrees that it is **waiving** all rights to offsets and liens pursuant to §29.

    • **has been settled** with the result that the Carrier/Self-insured is taking a credit of $_____ to resolve any rights to offsets and liens pursuant to §29.

    • has been settled and the settlement amount included in this agreement.

[15] There are occasions when the claimant has had a law suit in civil court. The optional paragraphs detail what is to happen with any of the money received by the claimant should the claimant win such a civil suit. For more details on third party law suits, go to page 87 in Chapter 11 - *Is the Money All Yours*.

Very often at the §32 settlement hearing, the claimant and/or the attorney are questioned as to the status of any open civil court or third party claims. If there are any questions about the status of these claims, the hearing could be adjourned so it is in the claimant's best interest to have current information on the case and make sure that both the claimant's attorney and the carrier know the name of the attorney handling that civil case if it is not the claimant's workers' compensation attorney. It is also appropriate to let the attorney in the civil case know that a workers' compensation claim has been filed and that a §32 settlement agreement is in process.

INCOME TAX

All sums set forth above constitute damages on account of personal injuries arising from an occurrence within the meaning of Section 104(a)(1) of the Interval Revenue Code.

This is done primarily for the benefit of the claimant's attorneys but with the changes in the tax code, it is essential that the claimant know the current tax codes in effect at the time the agreement is signed, as noted on page 87 in Chapter 11 - *Is the Money All Yours?*

LIENS

The claimant confirms that there are no liens for child support or alimony. See page 84 in Chapter 11 - *Is the Money All Yours?*

ENGLISH LANGUAGE

The claimant's attorney confirms that the claimant understands English and that there is no need for a translator to assist the claimant in understanding the terms and conditions of this agreement.

When I was doing §32's in New York, about 35% required a translator; I conducted hearings that were translated into over 50 languages. Sometimes, claimants who conducted all their meetings with their attorney and attended hearings at the Board without a translator would ask for one at the §32 hearing because they understood the importance and finality of the agreement. So, we would end up having to cross this paragraph out of the agreement at the hearing.

Translators, hired from outside firms, are certified in specific languages, except on occasions in which qualified Board staff act as translators. As a matter of policy, the claimant's family, friends, and even their attorney may not act as a translator; nor may a commissioner or a law judge.

GENERAL RELEASE

In consideration for this settlement, the claimant and the claimant's heirs, executors, administrators, trustees, legal representatives and assigns hereby forever releases and discharges the employer and carrier/Self-insured and any of their past or present entities, subsidiaries, divisions, affiliates, related business entities, successors and assigns and their respective heirs, executors, administrators, trustees, legal representatives and assigns, from all claims, demands, causes of action and liabilities that were or could have been raised in conjunction with WCB case #_____.

The above paragraph means that no one else, spouse, relative, creditor, etc can challenge the legality or contents of the §32 agreement, including the claimant's heirs or beneficiaries, should the claimant die after the §32 is approved.

NO OTHER ATTACHMENTS

The above constitutes the complete agreement of the parties for the resolution of all outstanding issues in the above Workers' Compensation claim(s) and the parties attest that there are no other documents or agreements on which the signing of this agreement is contingent.

These last two lines about *'other documents or agreements'* have always caused some difficulties for some carriers and/or employers. One upstate carrier would insist that the claimant sign either a letter of resignation or a letter agreeing to never seek employment with the employer again. The Board has categorically rejected any additional documents or contracts as being a part of the §32.

First, some of the documents that carriers or their employers wanted to attach to the §32 settlement dealt with legal issues outside the jurisdiction of the New York State Workers' Compensation Law. Some were in violation of union contracts or state laws and even possibly in violation of federal laws. Since the Board's jurisdiction is limited to Workers' Compensation Law, such attachments were not allowed. And any suggestion that there was such a *'hidden'* or *'secret'* agreement would result in the §32 being rejected and a note sent to the Board's general counsel for further investigation.

Second, the claimant is supposed to accept the settlement based on the terms of the agreement: a certain number of dollars to close the case. Other conditions, not in the actual §32, could be deemed to be unfair pressure or duress[23] on a claimant and the Board would not approve the agreement.

23... The Board uses the term 'duress' to mean improper pressure or threats or any kind.

In one case that came before me, a civil court judge in Brooklyn issued a court order instructing the claimant that, unless the claimant signed the §32 agreement, the judge would not allow a civil case involving the claimant to be settled. My position was that the civil court judge was exceeding his authority, interfering in workers' compensation law which was not within his jurisdiction, putting the claimant under improper pressure, and most importantly, had no authority to make me, as a commissioner, or any of the Board's law judges adhere to his instruction. Ultimately the civil court judge had to withdraw his court order.

The withdrawal of the court order enforced the Board's position that no conditions, other than those in the §32 settlement itself, can used as the basis of having the claimant sign the agreement.

There are occasions when another document, such as the annuity agreement or Medicare Set-Aside, is attached. But those are *'informational'* documents and, although sometimes read by the law judge/commissioner, are not considered when the §32 agreement is reviewed at the hearing. Thus the commissioner/law judge does not have the legal authority to rule on the legality of such attachments nor the formal training to do so, although they are within their right (and some feel their responsibility) to question the appropriateness of such attachments.

CLOSING PARAGRAPH

All parties agree that upon the approval of this settlement, the settlement will become final, irrevocable , and not subject to re-opening, reconsideration, or appeal except by written consent of both parties and approval of the Workers' Compensation Board. The claimant further agrees that the claimant will not apply to the Workers' Compensation Board for re-re-opening, reconsideration or appeal, notwithstanding any change in medical condition or earnings based upon the same common nucleus of operative facts which formed the basis of this claim. This settlement is final, conclusive and binding on all parties.

◆Hand written edits

Hand written notes on the agreement created a number of problems, although it was the official position of the Board when I was a commissioner that as long as everyone agreed to the settlement that was on paper, hand written notes were fine.

But several times, as the result of handwritten notes, the changes on one copy of the three copies of the agreement in the hearing part (claimant's copy, carrier's copy, and commissioner/law judge's copy) were not always the same. So when I asked the claimant if the agreement I had was identical to the agreement he had in front of him at the hearing, I would take my copy of the agreement, get up from my chair, walk around the table to where the claimant was sitting, and let him and both his attorney and the carrier's attorneys see what would become the official version, and then ask the claimant to confirm that it was his signature on the last page of the agreement I was holding.

Usually that would be the end of the matter but, on occasion, if there had been some changes to the agreement after one draft was done, either the carrier or claimant's attorney when asked to take a look at the copy I was holding, would state that the agreement that they brought with them to the hearing was different. If the copies were different, we could make the appropriate changes to my copy, which would become the one in the Board files and the only legal version of the agreement.

The same would hold true if I requested changes be made in the agreement, either because I changed the legal fee and/or clarified a site of injury or just some minor typo that no one else noticed. I would ask all three parties to sign and that is the copy I would sign, thus making this copy the official copy.

Equally important was the court reporter in the hearing part who was taking down not only all the conversations regarding these changes but everything that was said from when the hearing started to when it ended. This meant that there would be a written record available should questions arise sometime in the future.[24]

◆Summary

This generic agreement which I have drafted is a basic agreement.

Various law firms for both claimants and carriers have their own boiler plate format but the above basic text covers all the issues that should be addressed in whatever form the §32 is submitted to the claimant.

24...At this time, the Board is planning to replace the live court reporter with a tape record. How that will impact on the need for written copy of the hearing remains to be seen despite the Board's assurance that "Don't worry - the system will work."

Once both the claimant and the carrier have signed the agreement, it is sent to the Board and scheduled for a hearing. Although the claimant's attorney is asked to sign the agreement, the claimant's attorney's failure or refusal to do so does not affect the final approval or legality of this §32 agreement, as long as it is approved by a law judge or commissioner. Details on the actual hearing process can be found in Chapter 10 - _Hearings_ on page 78.

Other paragraphs may be added if there are unusual conditions or issues to be resolved in the settlement or some aspect of the case history that warrants inclusion. Those cases in which settlements may involve multiple employers and/or carriers/ and/or accidents may have additional clarifying language.

The important concept to understand is that there are thousands of settlements made every year. And while most are relatively simple and can be done with the same language, there is no '_one fits all_' agreement.

Whether these agreements are drafted by the claimants' attorneys or the carriers or the carriers' attorneys, it is important that the claimants understand that it is their life that is being covered by the agreement and it is their responsibility, with the assistance of their attorney, to make sure that the agreement is complete, correct, comprehensive, and fair.

CREDITCREDITCREDITCREDIT

Chapter 4
DO YOU NEED AN ATTORNEY?

◆Yes.

The alternative to being represented by an attorney is to be *pro se*: advocating on one's own behalf in a legal proceeding rather than being represented by an attorney.

If you fell on a sidewalk in front of a building owned by Donald Trump and broke your leg, would you accept an agreement from him, under which he will pay you for the six weeks you lost time at work and for all your medical bills without your checking with an attorney?

I do not think that you would do that. So why would you not get an attorney just because it is your employer or its carrier rather than Donald Trump?

§32's, in 99% of the cases, are quite similar, in that in exchange for, or as attorneys call it, '*in consideration of*', a certain sum of money, the claimant is agreeing to no longer pursue the legal right to seek additional monies for lost time or medical expenses from the party deemed to be responsible for causing the injury, even if the claimant has more problems in the future.

Now, as nice as the person may be who works for the carrier, and many of them are very nice, they do not represent the claimant. They represent the carrier. And they are responsible for helping the carrier minimize any expenses it may incur in the course of dealing with the claim. Also, the vast majority of the claims examiners are not attorneys. And while, in 99% of the cases, their recommendations to the claimant may make a lot of legal sense, there may be aspects of either the claimant's case or personal life which could impact or would be impacted by a §32 agreement in such a way that staff at the carrier may be not aware.

For those claimants who are either now on Medicare or Social Security Disability, or are seeking coverage under either, there are additional legal complications so complex that my experience showed that only attorneys who regularly deal with Medicare can keep up to date on its ever-changing laws.

Also, if the claimant has pending any third-party law suits, it is always possible that the §32 settlement may impact on it or *vice versa..*

Yes, while attorneys do charge money for their services, it is my opinion that the overwhelming majority of those who represent claimants in workers' compensation deserve the fees they request for the work they do. The answer to what is a fair fee is covered in Chapter 9 - *§32 Legal Fees* on page 72.

The purpose of this chapter, Chapter 4, is to answer the question of whether claimants need an attorney.

I am sure that anyone who has been in a §32 settlement hearing would report that the hearings are fairly '*cut and dry*', the hearings seem to be rather simple, and, for the most part, these reports are correct. However, the reason attorneys are hired prior to agreements being completed is not because there is going to be a problem, it is because with the assistance of the attorney, there will not be a problem at the hearing or in the future, and if there is, the agreement should be quite clear as to how that problem is going to be resolved. Also, no claimant wants the settlement delayed because some last minute problem came up at the hearing that the claimant does not understand whereas the attorney, if the claimant had one, could resolve that problem in two minutes.

And, although no one will admit to it, claimants' attorneys and licensed reps will coach the claimants as to how to respond to the questions asked of them at the hearing by the commissioner, law judge, and sometimes even the carrier's attorney. It is as important to know what to say as it is to know what NOT to say.

Effectively, the reason that most of these hearings appear to be so '*cut and dry*' is because the claimants' attorneys have worked out solutions to problems before the agreement is finalized.

◆Why can't you represent yourself?

There's an old saying, "*The lawyer who represents himself has a fool for a client.*" I do remember two occasions in which the injured party was an attorney. They both decided to represent themselves: one was a licensed representative dealing exclusively in workers' compensation and the other was an attorney in general practice. Both of their performances were an embarrassment and I personally think that, by representing themselves, their cases and arguments were not as well presented as they may have been had they hired an experienced workers' compensation attorney or licensed represenative. As to whether or not they both lost their cases as a result of the facts of the case or their inability to make a proper presentation is a determination I leave to others.

However, it has been my experience over the years, and I have served on a variety of boards in the political, commercial, and not-for-profit fields, that while I may be able to negotiate on my own and work out many of the details, when it comes to the formal agreement itself, I always hired an attorney. And the attorney, more often than not, would find some small item I had either neglected to include or was unaware of. It is their business to keep up-to-date on all new laws, rules and regulations, and court cases that can affect an agreement. They also know all the law judges, examiners, and opposing counsel and therefore know best how to communicate with them. And this can not be done by becoming an *attorney* for one day or one project.

◆Do you need a specialist or just a general attorney?

It is important to get an attorney who has experience with workers' compensation law. While many personal injury attorneys can handle a workers' compensation claim, unless they do a lot of workers' compensation, the claimants usually have better representation with an attorney who specializes in the workers' compensation field.

In addition, in New York State, there is a class of individuals called Licensed Representatives (WCL §24-a). Having passed a very vigorous test administered by the NYS Board (about 90% of applicants fail the test), these licensed representatives are authorized to handle all aspects of a workers' compensation claim. The vast majority are not only as good as any attorney experienced in the workers' compensation field but are also far better in handling a workers' compensation case than any attorney who does not regularly practice workers' compensation.

And for this reason, throughout the rest of this book, whenever I refer to *attorney*, I also mean *licensed representative*. if there are exceptions it will be duly noted.

◆Where can you find a qualified attorney?

The NYS Board has a list of licensed reps on their web site:

www.wcb.state.ny.us/content/main/Reps/LisRepListing-Sec24a.pdf

For an attorney in the field, an excellent list is available from the New York Workers' Compensation Alliance:

www.nyworkerscompensationalliance.org

or the Injured Workers Bar Association
http://www.injuredworkersbar.org/Find-An-Attorney

To be blunt, **you should get an attorney**.

You do not want to be the one person for whom what appeared to be a simple agreement turns out not to be and now you find yourself in civil court, spending thousands of dollars to resolve something that could have been easily prevented had you had an attorney help you with your §32.

As to the question of how much do they charge, the answers will be in Chapter 9 - *§32 Legal Fees* on page 72.

And one last point, before moving on in this book. You are hiring an attorney or licensed representative for his advice based on your attorney's years of experience in the workers' compensation field. Your attorney is not there to agree with you on everything, tell you what you want to hear, or guarantee that you will 'win', although your attorney will try to do all three. Your attorney is there to make sure that you will get the most compensation and best medical treatment possible under the limitations of the workers' compensation system.

CRBOCRBOCRBOCRBO

Chapter 5
ISSUES RESOLVED BY §32'S

When the concept of the §32 settlement was first envisioned in New York State prior to becoming incorporated into the law in September 1996, it was expected that these new settlements would replace the Lump Sum Settlements that were done under WCL §15–5(b).

In late 1997, when the §32 agreements started coming across the desks of the commissioners, the types of cases settled by the §32's were basically the same as those types of cases closed under the §15-5(b) cases: virtually all the claimants has been classified as having a PPD. But after about six months, we started getting cases in which the issues were degrees of disability and rates of compensation; occasionally there were cases in which the issue was a 'C-7'[25], whether the case should be accepted or disallowed.

In reality the §32 settlement is an agreement which allows the parties to take any issue which is being controverted and use the §32 to settle only one issue[26] or then entire case.

Many years ago I proposed that the Workers' Compensation Board set up some sort of a website in which unusual cases could be posted so that, when a problem was resolved in New York City, an attorney in Buffalo would not have to reinvent the wheel. I also proposed that there be a question-and-answer page on the website for attorneys who had unusual issues to be resolved. As was the case with virtually all the suggestions made by not only me, but also all the other commissioners, this proposal ended up in the circular file. In Chapter 18 - <u>§32 Settlements</u> of my book, <u>Behind The Closed Doors</u>, I referenced cases in which compensation and medical treatment were not subject to dispute.[27]

25...The C-7 is a Board-issued form that carriers must submit if they object to the entirety of the claim or any portion of it.

26...The settlement of just one issue while the balance of the case remains open is sometimes considered a Stipulation. More on that later on page 48 in this chapter.

27...Details on my earlier book, <u>Behind The Closed Doors: An insider's look at how things really work at the NYS Workers Compensation Board -And how to fix them</u> can be found on page 152.

◆WAMO Waiver Agreement Management Office

The 2007 Workers' Compensation Reform legislation mandated that the NYS Workers' Compensation Board (Board) Chair establish a Waiver Agreement Management Office (WAMO), ". . . *to negotiate and seek Board approval for waiver agreements on behalf of the special disability fund.*" [WCL §32(e)]. (See Appendix D - <u>WAMO Guidelines</u> on page 123.) But in reality, the goal of WAMO, according to the Board's own publication, is to *"greatly reduce or eliminate the annual assessments against self-insured employers, insurance carriers and the State Insurance Fund . . ."* and *"all of which will aid in greatly reducing or eliminating assessments."* Nowhere in this document is there any indication that WAMO or any other department of the Board has an interest in making sure that the claimant understands the implications of a §32 settlement. As the Board memo states, the purpose of WAMO is to act on behalf of the Special Disability Fund, one of many funds managed by the State and supported by carrier-mandated payments to cover certain cost for workers' compensation claims. In some cases, these *'funds'* are the only ones signing the agreement with the claimant. See page 92 in Chapter 12 - <u>Who Participates in the agreement?</u>

Yes, there is a list of items that the Board must review under its WAMO guidelines but these are designed primarily to make sure that the agreement is approved by the Board, not to insure that the claimants have a complete or even minimal understanding of what the agreement means to them in the future.

◆Samples of issues that can be resolved

What follows are some of the types of disputes that were resolved by §32 agreements, offered here in the expectation that all the practitioners and the claimants will realize how many different types of problems can be resolved, whether they relate to the entirety of the case or just to one particular issue.

Equally important, there are a few issues which can not be included in a §32 settlement. These are listed at the end of this chapter.

Two widows
There were two women fighting over who was the legal widow of the deceased injured worker. The deceased Russian immigrant had married one of the women in Canada and the second woman in the United States

and there was a question as to the validity of his divorce from the Canadian wife as well as that marriage itself. The Board's Office of the General Counsel said that there could not be a §32 settlement until an administrative law judge picked one of the women as the legal heir, which was the one issue both women wished to avoid by the settlement. The other issue is that one of the women had a son by the deceased and neither woman wanted to deprive that son of his benefits which could happen if the mother was not deemed the surviving spouse[28].

I disagreed with the General Counsel arguing, in part, that there could have been an earlier wife in Russia, that if this case went before a law judge who decided which of these two women was the wife, and the story got into any Russian language newspapers, a third woman, possibly an earlier wife, living in Russia, could appear. I spoke to the attorneys for both women and the carrier and the §32 was drafted with language which stated that the dispute between the two women would be resolved with a shared payment to both. No decision as to which was the legal widow was in the agreement and the carrier understood that if a woman from Russia came forward claiming to be the first and yet-to-be divorced wife that the carrier may have to pay her, too, although that payment would not affect the agreement and the monies paid to the two women and the child. All agreed; the case was settled.

Illegal employment of a minor
In this case the claimant was about 20 years old but he been injured about six years earlier at which time it was found that the employer was in violation of WCL §14a: the claimant was illegally employed as a minor. As a result of that finding, pursuant to the WCL §14a, when the awards were made to the claimant by the carrier, the employer also had to pay an equal amount to the claimant as his penalty for the illegal employment although it was the carrier and not the employer who was responsible for medical bills. In this particular case, the carrier and the claimant wanted to settle the claim but the employer had no interest and/or was unable to do so.

As a result, the agreement was drafted in such a way that the carrier closed its case with the claimant by a one-time payment which also included an unspecified amount for potential future medical expenses, as only the carrier was responsible for the medical treatment. Therefore, the

---

28...Although children born of out wedlock can qualify for workers compensation benefits, proving that fact can be a complex and time-consuming battle.

only portion of the case which remained open was that portion under which the illegal employer was responsible for continuing to pay compensation to the claimant as long as the claimant met the necessary standards of disability which had been previously established.

Life-long medical account
Another case involved a young dancer who, while traveling with her dance company overseas, got a mosquito bite to her leg causing an infection that basically destroyed her immune system as well as her ability to dance. The issue of compensation was relatively simple and she ended up with the compensation payment portion of the award to her satisfaction.

However, because of the unique nature of her illness, it was realized that something as simple as a scratch or a minor cold could result in serious if not fatal medical complications such that, on any of these occasions, she would have to immediately go to the emergency room of the nearest hospital and to be put into a critical care unit. The potential medical costs for such treatment were such that the carrier did not want to write out a check for hundreds of thousands of dollars in the event that this did become necessary.

The result was an agreement in which a sum of $25,000 a year was put into a special escrow account under the claimant's control specifically for medical expenses relating to this condition. In addition each year the carrier would pay up to the first $25,000 for any medical expenses incurred by this claimant as a result of this medical condition with all other expenses that year to come from the medical escrow account or any other financial resources to which the claimant had access. Both sides felt that this was fair and equitable, the agreement signed, and the case closed.

Special medical treatment
The claimant came to the hearing with an agreement under the terms of which the carrier would pay every few years for the total cost of purchasing and fitting a prosthetic arm for the claimant who had lost his arm up to the shoulder. During the hearing when I asked the claimant where his prosthetic arm was, he stated that he was going in for the final fitting of this first prosthetic arm in about two weeks. I suggested to him that perhaps he should wait for a few weeks until after he had this done. I explained my reasoning: as long as the carrier still had an open claim with him, if he had any problems with the prosthetic arm, he would know

that he would have a very large carrier behind him, to make sure that the prosthetic fit. Once it was fit and he was satisfied, then it would make more sense for him to come to the hearing knowing that everything was fine. And then he could settle this case. All the parties agreed and the case was formally closed at a hearing a few months later.

Missing checks

At the final hearing for this claimant, she complained that, in the past year, some of her checks had gone missing. I adjourned the case for an investigation and rescheduled the case 60 days later, expecting that the issue would have been resolved. It was, that is, for the missing checks from the prior hearings.,But now she complained that two checks sent to her since the last hearings were missing. When it was suggested that we adjourn again, I said *"No, as I have a sense that there will be missing checks every time we have a hearing and we will never get this settlement approved."* I proposed there be a short recess for the attorneys (claimant's and carrier's) to write a short addendum to the agreement which state that the only one issue would remain open: the matter of the missing checks. This issue would be decided by the Board under its continuing jurisdiction. This not only limited the number of missing checks to those referenced at the hearing but allowed the settlement to go forward, and be approved. I was told that it took about six months to learn that a member of her family was responsible for the checks disappearing. But after that issue was resolved, the claim was formally finished and the §32 agreement long since approved.

Death claims

Under the current Workers' Compensation Law, when a worker's death is accepted as a death claim, either as a direct result of an accident or complications arising at a later date, if there is a surviving spouse, that spouse continues to receive the decedent's benefits.

In these cases, a new claim - a death claim - is established with the claimant now being the surviving spouse or the executor of the estate.

This does get a bit more complex if there is a question about some possible weeks of compensation due the claimant that the carrier did not pay before the claimant died. If it is found that additional compensation was due to the claimant for time lost before his death, WCL §2(8) indicates that there may still be an award due to the claimant's estate after his death. A new file is opened with the surviving spouse or executor of the estate as the new '*claimant*'. Since this claim in the injury case for the time lost from work for which weekly awards were still being controverted or just not yet awarded is still open, when it comes time to settle the §32, there are actually two '*claimants*'. I always insisted that both sign the agreement if both cases are being closed, even if it is the same person signing in two places; they are signed in two capacities: of the estate and widow(er).

While some, including some of the legal staff at the Board, considered my policy ridiculous, there were occasions when there were in fact two different claimants. In one case, the decedent was in the process of getting a divorce from his wife but died before the divorce could be completed. But, in his will, he left his entire estate to his '*significant other*' and made her the executrix of the estate. In the death claim, his '*significant other*' had an legal claim for the benefits due prior to his death, but his wife had a claim for the lump sum death benefit. Hence I required two signatures.

For these and several other unusual cases, it is not possible to even suggest what is fair. Again, an attorney who can talk to other attorneys in the workers' compensation field can make suggestions to the claimant as to what may be a reasonable settlement for the issues involved.

Claimant dies at time of settlement
Although it is a rare occurrence, there have been times when a claimant died prior to the settlement being formally approved by the Board. In a March 2, 2000 Board decision in the *Matter of Anchor Motor Freight, 2000 NY Wrk. Comp. 57903606; 2000 NY Wrk. Comp. LEXIS 108384*, the claimant died just before the Notice of Approval of the agreement was filed. The carrier's attorney contended that, since the claimant died prior to the lump sum settlement being approved by the Board, neither the claimant's spouse nor estate were entitled to the lump sum settlement or to any benefits beyond his date of death. The Board Panel agreed, writing in its decision that, "*Where the claimant dies prior to the lump sum settlement being approved by the Board, neither the claimant nor his estate is entitled to the lump sum settlement.*" The Board decision was based on a decision issued in 1956 by the New York State Court of Appeals, in *the Matter of Zielinski v. General Motors Corp.,1 N.Y.2d 424; 135 N.E.2d 808; 153 N.Y.S.2d 642(1956)*. Although this case dealt with the older '*lump sum settlements*' under §15-5b, it is more than reasonable to expect that if a claimant dies before the §32 agreement is

signed by the law judge/commissioner, the settlement will be voided.

Therefore, those claimants whose ill health is one of the reasons they are seeking a settlement for their claim(s) should take heed of the importance of time in completing their settlement.

Minor children

In some cases, there are surviving children or dependents, defined as under the age of 18, attending a college until the age of 23, or severely handicapped.[29]

> If the spouse remarries, the spouse qualifies for a one-time payment and the case is closed.
> If there are dependents, 45% of the weekly award is apportioned to them and the payments to the surviving spouse are reduced by that amount, netting the surviving spouse 55%.
> If the surviving spouse remarries but has children, the payments to the dependents continue. If there are two dependents, it will increase to 37.5% each from the original 22.5% each (the original 45% ÷ 2 dependents); if there are three dependents it will increase to 33.33% from the original 15% (the original 45% ÷ 3 dependents).

In these cases, there is a question as to whether or not the surviving spouse can settle not only their claim but the claim of the dependents as well. In some cases, the interest of the surviving spouse and the dependents are considered to be the same. In other cases, the interest of the surviving spouse may be not only different but in opposition to that of the dependents. And there are the cases in which the dependents are not the children of the surviving spouse but are from an earlier marriage or even out of wedlock. In these cases, a third party would be designated to determine if the dependents should take a settlement. In fact, that third party may even be able to negotiation an entirely different settlement for these dependent children.

Another issue arises because under WCL §16(2), individuals as old as 22

29...Such issues as a 20-year-old leaving college and then going back at age 21 or severely handicapped children over 18 are complex and require an attorney to explain them in relationship to the specifics of the claim. Also after 9/11, certain definitions were modified to increase or decease benefits for the families of those who died as a result of that terrorist attack.

can be considered to be '*dependent*' and continue to receive workers' compensation benefits. Yet under the law, once they reach the age of 18, not only do the parents or guardians no longer have any right to sign contracts on their behalf, these individuals now have the legal right to negotiate and sign contracts on their own.[30] Therefore, if the surviving spouse wishes to settle a claim by a §32 settlement and has a child over the age of 18 who is receiving benefits, there are two parties who must sign the agreement as recipient of funds. As to whether or not they should be represented by the same attorney or the surviving spouse can use a Power of Attorney from the dependents is an issue that should be cleared before the hearing with the Board's Office of the General Counsel and this clearance confirmed to the law judge/commissioner during the settlement hearing.

Claims involving fraud
In 1996, when the workers' compensation law was amended, WCL §114 was modified with WCL §114-a. §114 considered fraud in the workers' compensation system to be a criminal offence, which meant that it could only be prosecuted by the district attorney in whose county the alleged fraud took place. The amendment, WCL §114-a, made fraud a civil offence, thus giving the Board power to look into the alleged fraud, bring the issue to a trial (at the Board), and issue a finding and penalties. And, as a result of the Board having completed the investigation and even a hearing during which §114-a fraud was found, many district attorneys would then take the case and pursue a §114 criminal fraud conviction. In a civil case, the carrier or employer can do all the investigation whereas in a criminal case, it is only the office of the local district attorney whose limited resources, prior to the 1996 amendment, meant that these types of insurance fraud cases were not prosecuted.

Suddenly, a number of carriers, in particular one in upstate New York, charged every claimant with fraud in order to force them into accepting whatever that carrier wanted.

As a result the Board started to get cases in which fraud was one of the open issues. As noted on page 29 in Chapter 3 - *A Basic Agreement*, the Board considered this as '*duress*' and rejected every agreement. The Board decided that the fraud issue could only be noted in the §32

30...Those dependents who are over 18 but for reasons noted in the preceding footnote may require a guardian and therefore may also require separate legal representation.

agreement if the claimant had been found guilty of same, either §114 or §114-a. Otherwise, it had no place in the agreement. Also, the fraud issue had to be resolved <u>before</u> the §32 hearing so there would be no question that it played any part in the claimant's decision to accept the agreement.

Under the Board's procedures, the commissioners could not make decisions at the settlement hearing on the facts already established in the case; they could only approve or disapprove the agreement or make some minor changes. Therefore, they could not at the §32 hearing make a decision that there was no fraud. The carrier had to appear separately before a law judge and withdraw the claim of fraud *'with prejudice'*[31] so that it could never be raised again, even if the claimant rejected the §32 after the allegations of fraud were dropped.

One time, the carrier agreed at a hearing to cross out a sentence in the agreement which referenced the alleged fraud, agreeing to cross it out because the carrier had a few days earlier learned that fraud did not happen. I told the carrier, as well as the claimant and his attorney, that I would not accept the agreement. I stated,

> *The agreement is a formal legal document that the claimant may meed to present to others in the future. The fact that the word is crossed out means that these words referencing fraud are still in the agreement and can be read and have a negative impact on people's perception of the claimant. So go before a law judge, withdraw the fraud allegation, with prejudice, rewrite the agreement, and come back here next week.*

The only time that the Board would accept the reference to fraud or §114 or §114-a was when there was a finding that the claimant was guilty of same and that fraud was one of the considerations in settling the claim. I did have one agreement in which under the §32 agreement, the claimant agreed to repay the carrier the $47,000 the claimant received while committing §114-a fraud.

Therefore, if there is an open fraud claim pending, it must be resolved, with prejudice, before the Board will allow a §32 to go forward. It can not be used to pressure a claimant into accepting an agreement the claimant would have otherwise rejected.

31...'*With prejudice*' means that the matter or issue is closed and can not be raised again.

Discrimination under §120
Under §120 of the New York State Workers' Compensation Law, it is possible for injured workers to bring a claim of discrimination against their employer. However, the definition of '*discrimination*' is strictly defined in Workers' Compensation Law as any act of discrimination against employees because they have in the past or may in the future file a claim for compensation and/or act as a witness for another injured worker. In one case during an oral argument, my panel told one claimant that even if she were discriminated against because of her age, gender, and nationality, this form of discrimination is not covered by workers' compensation law but by laws administered by other state and federal agencies.

The inclusion of §120 discrimination in this book is to advise those interested in seeking a settlement that issues relating to §120 can be settled with a §32 agreement. And, if there is also an open claim for injuries, these both can be consolidated into one agreement.

◆Issues that can not be resolved

Sites of injury
Once a site of injury has been established, the §32 agreement can not '*disallow*' that site of injury. The agreement can only '*disallow*' sites of injuries that have been disputed and thus have not yet been established or disallowed.

Quitting, resigning, or retiring
The claimant, whether or not the compensation case has been established, can not be required to promise to leave their current job as a condition for getting the §32 settlement. This also means that there can be no '*secret*' addendum to the §32 agreement which makes this demand of the claimant.

Reapplying for employment
The claimant, whether or not the case has been established, can not be required to promise not to re-apply to the former employer for a job. This also means that there can be no '*secret*' addendum to the §32 agreement which makes this demand of the claimant. WCL §125 prohibits an employer to discriminate against any worker seeking employment who has an open workers' compensation claim or has closed one with a §32 agreement. From a practical perspective, what would happen if the

claimant agreed not to reapply for employment with Company A. Later Company A is bought out by or buys Company B? Would this prevent the claimant from seeking employment with Company B? And if already employed at Company B would the claimant then have to resign?

Make a third party part of the agreement
The §32 agreement can not require that a third party, i.e., spouse, employer, medical provider, etc., perform some act or not perform some act and this includes Medicare. The only parties who are required to follow the terms of the agreement are the '*interested parties*', the claimant and the carrier. See page 92 for Chapter 12 - *Who Participates in The Agreement?*

Other jurisdictions
The §32 agreement can not be subject to approval in some other jurisdiction (i.e. federal, another state or country or another judicial system such as Supreme Court [civil or criminal] or OEEC, etc.) The New York State Workers' Compensation Board does not have the authority to enforce rules, laws, and/or regulations of other authorities. Neither the Board, the commissioners, nor law judges have formal knowledge of the rules, laws, and/or regulations of other authorities' laws. Hence such language is inappropriate in a settlement agreement and thus not allowed. This is another reason that the language regarding quitting, resigning or not seeking re-employment are not allowed to be in a §32 agreement or as an attachment,

Future injuries or claims
The §32 agreement can not have any reference to or be a general release for any and all other claims for injuries or occupational disease that may not yet have been filed or that may occur in the future and would be considered a new claim rather than a continuation of an existing claim. The agreement's language must relate specifically only to the case(s) specifically being settled, and listed by case number, in the agreement.

There have been cases of claimants who have severe occupational diseases whose life expectancy is relatively short. In the early days when they negotiated the §32 settlement, some carriers attempted to include language that in effect said that, if the claimant dies as the result of the injury or occupational disease covered by the agreement, there could be no claim for death benefits. Such language was not allowed in the agreement for the simple reason that, were the claimant to become deceased as a result of the occupational disease or severe injury complications, the death claim would not be placed by the signatory to the §32, the now deceased claimant but would be placed a third-party, i.e., the surviving spouse, dependent, or the estate, and, under the law, the claimant in signing a §32 cannot sign away someone else's rights, i.e., the surviving spouse, dependent, or the estate.

However, in some cases, the carrier may insist that such language be in the agreement, the claimant signs the agreement, and the law judge/commissioner makes no mention this set of terms in the agreement of the during the hearing. As to whether or not a claim for death benefits by the survivors would be accepted by the Board and/or the courts is an issue which has yet to come before the Board or the courts.

◆Settling a claim versus keeping it open

I interviewed thousands of claimants who said they were taking the §32 to '*get out of the system*'. No more having someone looking over their shoulder. Now they can return to work. Some claimants do not like to leave the workers' compensation system as they like the financial security of (1) regular tax free payment and (2) not having family members or relatives asking for a '*gift*' from the newly '*rich*' claimant.

Claimants who do not settle their claims also like the knowledge that their medical expenses will be paid for without having to deal with private health insurance or Medicare. And, if they took a settlement, they would have to account for every dollar of the Medicare set-aside that they spend on work-place-injury-medical treatment to prove to Medicare that they have spent it all. (see Chapter 13 - *Medicare*, page 98) Because until the claimant can prove how all the set-aside was spent, Medicare will fight not to pay for any of the work-related medical expenses. And other health insurance providers will do the same: fight not to pay any medical expenses that in any way could be attributed to that work-place injury covered by the §32 agreement.

◆Stipulations

Under Workers' Compensation Law (NYCRR §300.5), "*[p]arties to any claim before the Board may stipulate to uncontested facts or proposed findings.*" The stipulation is an agreement between parties to resolve a specific issue but can not be used to settle an entire claim. Stipulations can settle the issue of average weekly wage, sites of injury, specific periods of lost time, or any other specific facts under dispute that related to past events..

There is one issue that can not be resolved by a stipulation: the claimant can not stipulate to any condition which limits their right to future medical treatment nor can it include statements with such language as *"there was also a finding of no further causally related disability to the head, neck and back."*

Also, it is possible to challenge a stipulation, although the Board and courts rarely invalidate a stipulation. But there is always the possibility.

Since many controverted issues deal with continuing medical problems or the possibility that a major medical issue may arise sometime in the future, and since both parties want to close the case without any possibility of it being reopened, the preference is to resolve differences with a §32.

It is possible to use a modified §32 to resolve differences that have in the past been done by a stipulation but, for the most part, carriers prefer to close the entire case whenever possible.

◆Summary

The §32 agreement is nothing more than an agreement that has been reached by the two parties to settle either the entirety of a claim or some specific issues, so that the parties can bring the matter(s) to a close.

What I found interesting during my term of office as a commissioner is that very often disputes over minor issues would delay cases for months if not for years. Perhaps the use of a limited §32 agreement with a few dollars on the table would result in some of these minor issues being resolved, allowing the balance of the claim to move toward its appropriate conclusion.

CRUCRUCRUCRU

Chapter 6
WHAT IS A GOOD DOLLAR VALUE

That is an easy one to answer: an amount that satisfies you.

I have seen settlements ranging from the claimant returning $47,000[32] (see page 45) to the carrier to a claimant receiving just over $9,000,000 (yes, million). And each was fair for the case that was being settled.

Basically, there are two components used by the carrier to determine what the carrier would be willing to pay you to settle your claim:

– COMPENSATION AND MEDICAL EXPENSES –

Because there are different types of cases. I will not give a lengthy analysis of what these are because you will recognize the group that you are in and therefore the other categories will be irrelevant for you.

- Claims established and claimant classified or will be classified as part of the §32 agreement.
- Claims established but compensation rate not yet fixed.
- Claims established but degree of disability and/or necessary medical care not yet determined.
- Claims being controverted, i.e., not yet established that there was an accident or that the carrier/employer is responsible under the workers' compensation law.
- Other: death claims, fraud, underage employment.

Other items for you to take into account are:

Do you have a job lined up after you take your settlement that the carrier is unaware of? You do not have to volunteer that information but you should speak to your attorney as to what to say if you are asked this question at the hearing. For, if you had taken that job before the settlement, your current weekly compensation awards would have been stopped or reduced. As a result, your settlement would be smaller. But to lie about having a job lined up or having just started back at work could result in a claim of fraud by the carrier with the possibility of a forfeiture of your entire settlement and the possibility of the loss of any future awards.

32...see page 45 for details on this 'refund'.

You just inherited $1,000,000 and plan to live the good life and do not want the bother of dealing with periodic visits from the carrier who wants to know if you have returned to work and, if not, why not, or maybe your disability has decreased.

You are planning to move out of the U.S. to a country that provides free medical care for any reason so you can use the medical set-aside for anything you want.

You have just found out you have a medical condition, unrelated to your work injury, that may shorten you life substantially and a five-year settlement offer is better than your projected life expectancy, but the carrier does not know this.[33]

And you may have a dozen other reasons for taking a settlement offer rather than staying in the system, pressuring you to take an offer lower than you might have taken if you could 'take it or leave it'. The following items assume that there is no 'hidden' or 'secret' reason for taking the settlement, just a desire to end your relationship with the Board, the carrier, and the system in general, a reason most often cited by claimants who appeared before me to close their cases forever.

– COMPENSATION –

◆Established and claimant classified

This category of cases has a lot of similarity with the Lump Sums discussed in detail in Chapter 2- *How did §32's Start?* starting on page 12.

Your rate of compensation has been fixed and, for the most part, medical treatment has stopped because your condition has stabilized. For purposes of this exercise, let us assume that your weekly award is $300.

The carrier knows that it will have to pay you $300 a week for a few years or maybe the rest of your life, unless you return to work at a wage equal to or higher than that being earned at the time of the original injury. That comes out to $15,600 a year. The carrier has insurance statistics including statistics from their own case files to guesstimate how much

33...See Appendix C, page 135 for an explanation and sample of a Life Expectancy Table

longer you will be getting this compensation rate: a function of your age, general health, and the possibility of your returning to work, at a higher, the same, or lower wage rate. The carrier enters all these numbers into a formula which tells them how the total amount they can expect to pay out to you in the future if you not take the settlement.

But, before you calculate $15,600 a year for five years and get $78,000, be aware that there is a financial formula used by bank and insurance companies which deals with the financial term called present cash value (PCV).[34] That is one of the formulas used by carrier to determine how much cash they must set aside in a '*reserve*' to make sure that they have enough to pay you. If they overestimate, they keep the difference; if they underestimate, they must pay you anyway.

But you can see that $300 a week for five years is not going to cost the carrier $78,000 and they are not going to give you anything more than that.

As a guide, most of the lump sums under WCL §15-5b were for five years worth of payments and that has carried over to the §32s for claimants who have been classified PPD or PTD. Is that fair? Who knows - that's just how it is done.

But if you had a heart attack last year, they will assume you will live less than their average and offer you less. If you do not think the revised offer is fair, reject it, and live longer. It is all about '*odds*' and statistical probabilities.

◆ATF (Aggregate Trust Fund)

On November 16, 2011, the New York State Court of Appeals issued a decision in *The Matter of Raynor v Landmark Chrysler* which, in effect, stated that, when a claimant was classified as having a permanent partial disability, the carrier was required to make a deposit into the ATF based on the present cash value of future payments. In order to calculate the amount of these payments, the carrier is supposed to use a number of

---

34...In order to have $100 in two years, if the current interest rate is 4%, you would have to invest only $92.46 while you would earn $7.54 in interest over the next two years so that you would have a total of $100. Hence the PCV of $100 in two years is $92.46 and the PCV of $100 in 10 years would be $64.96. So the cost to the carrier of giving you $100 in 10 years is $64.96 not $100.

tables provided by the Workers' Compensation Board and the State Insurance Fund. Basically, the younger the claimant the higher the amount that had to be deposited.

For example, for someone who is sixty years old the deposit had to be equal to 10 years' worth of payments.

Therefore, it would seem that when the 60-year-old claimant who had a permanent partial disability was negotiating with the carrier, the claimant would know that the carrier had a potential liability of 10 years and the claimant would not have to accept an offer of only five years but ask for the full 10 years' worth of compensation.

This is not as simple as it seems.

First of all, the State Insurance Fund, which accounts for 40% of all the cases in New York State, does not have to make the deposit. Therefore, it could offer five years as a "*take it or leave it*" offer. Also those companies who were self-insured, such as Verizon and Con Edison, also did not have to make the deposit and, therefore, could also offer five years as a "*take it or leave it*" offer.

At the time of the _Raynor_ decision, it was rumored that the ATF was only going to offer settlements with four or five years of compensation. [There is an issue regarding the balance of funds that were deposited by a carrier on a specific claim but not fully used for settlement. Who gets to keep the unspent money? It is my opinion that the answers to this may impact on the amount of deposits, refunds to carriers, and offers to claimants.]

Therefore, while the ATF ruling may appear to set a much higher settlement level for claimants whose compensation and medical payments have been paid for by private carriers than for settlements offered by the State Insurance Fund and self-insureds, this is a matter still being resolved.

The complexity of this issue and the various methods of calculating these values are further proof that the use of an attorney or a licensed representative in negotiating a §32 settlement is the prudent decision to make.

◆Mortality Tables

One key element used by the carrier (including the State Insurance Fund and the self-insured) in determining the amount of money they will offer you is what is know as a Mortality Table. These tables, issued by various government agencies and non-for-profit groups, list the age expectancy of everyone by their year of birth, broken down by sex, race, and dozens of other factors. It should be obvious that, if two people are in good health for their age and one is 30 years old and the other 60 years old, the 30-year-old will live more years from today than the 60-year-old. For the carrier that means the 30-year-old will collect more weekly payments and have more medical treatment over the claimant's life time. Fair . . . maybe not but that is life. More details and a sample of the Federal Government's Social Security Administration's Mortality Table will be found in Appendix G - *Mortality Tables*, on page 135.

◆Established but compensation rate not yet fixed

A lot of what is referenced in the two sections above applies to cases like this group except that the weekly dollar amount of compensation is unknown or there may be a temporary rate. If the case continues, there are four possible results that can occur:

> The temporary rate can be made permanent
> The temporary rate can be made permanent but at a higher rate
> The temporary rate can be made permanent but at a lower rate
> The compensation could be stopped together.

Only you and your attorney can make a judgement as to which of these four results may occur and thus these additional variables and risk factors will have to go into your calculations as to how much is fair.

◆Controverted, i.e., not yet established

If you were to get your case established and then get awards, you would have a better idea of what you would be giving up if you take a settlement, which in these cases need not be very small. But on the other hand, you could lose your case and get nothing. Once again, your attorney can help you review all the possibilities and help make a decision. And while these settlements are usually small for most claims, those without serious medical problems, the small settlement should be acceptable. And you can get out of the system.

◆Claim established but degree of disability and/or necessary medical care not yet determined

The degree of disability is usually translated into a dollar amount for the weekly awards: the higher the disability, the higher the weekly pay rate. But over time, as the condition improves (hopefully), the degree of disability decreases, so also does the rate of compensation and the cost to the carrier to settle the claim. The value of such settlements is more fully covered in the next section

◆Established but compensation rate not yet fixed

But when the major issue is medical care, there are a lot of variables. The carrier, with industry and its own statistics, has an estimate of how much it will have to set aside into a '*reserve*' fund to pay for your future medical treatment. If you settle, they will do calculations on that '*reserve*', come up with a PCV, and add that to the amount it calculated for the compensation.

If it feels the medical expenses will decrease, the carrier will offer you less than if it sees surgery or major complications somewhere in the future. You have to take these considerations into account as well. But the value of medical expenses in any settlement is a complex subject and has warranted an entire chapter, which starts after this one.

◆Some prior settlements as a guide

Yes, I had a case in which the settlement was for about $9,000,000. Virtually the entire sum was for medical expenses for a young person who was a paraplegic who had a long life expectancy. These funds were put into a special account to cover his 24-hour medical care. Most of the large 6- and 7-figure settlements have a very large medical component. Before you wonder why you can not get such a large settlement, consider the severity of the life-long disability from which these claimants suffer in order to qualify for such large awards, virtually all for medical treatment.

And of course, we all know of the friend of a friend who got $50,000 when he lost his finger in an accident. So why can't you get the same amount? Which finger did that person lose and which finger did you lose? Was he a professional musician and you are a clerk, because he may have lost his livelihood but you did not? And maybe there were severe medical complications and a lot of that money is for future medical care whereas your hand has fully healed. [35]

You cannot compare one person's settlement with another as there are many factors that determine the amount of the settlement and it is unlikely that your case and that other person's injuries and medical history are identical.

Also, you may get an offer for $50,000 and reject it. Then a few years later, discussions open again and the offer is for $40,000. *"Why lower?"*, you ask. Well, you are a few years older, hence a shorter life expectancy. Also, the carrier has a much better idea of your future medical expenses and it is most likely that all the larger expenses were incurred in the few years after you rejected the first offer. And finally, most likely, this time, it is you who is asking for a settlement. As in all business and personal dealings, he who asks is already at a disadvantage.

◆Summary

As you can read, the answer to *"What is Fair?"* is very complex. It differs for everybody and changes for each claimant over time.

To this day, there is still a question as to whether or not §32's are fair to claimants. In upholding a controversial redistricting plan in January 6, 2004 a three-judge federal court in Austin, Texas ruled,

> *"We decide only the legality of (the plan), not its wisdom. Whether the Texas Legislature has acted in the best interest of Texas is a judgment that belongs to the people who elected those officials whose act is challenged in this case."*

The same could be said for §32's in New York: as long as the Legislature allows them and the agreements meet the WCB's interpretation of the law, the Board is required to give them an honest review.

Essentially the carrier calculates what it will cost to settle and what it will cost to keep your case open. No emotions, just dollars. Understand that

---

35... Anyone who has diabetes knows that what may be a simple injury and a simple recovery for non-diabetics can sometimes be very complex and involve serious and costly medical complications for a diabetic.

each carrier has its own formulas and confidential methods of calculating these numbers, with the result that offers for '*identical*' cases may vary. And different carriers with the same identical case may have somewhat different numbers.

The key consideration for you to think about is:

> If you look back three or more years from now, will you feel that you made the right decision?

Monday morning quarter-backing works great for TV sports but not in real life. It is your life on the line, your future. You have an attorney who has experience with these settlements, and you can only make the best decision you can after discussing with your attorney all the facts and options that you have at hand.

If the agreement feels fair, then it is. And if doesn't feel fair, don't take it. You must remember that it is your life and your decision about what is best for you. Do not let your friends or relatives interfere with your making a decision that is correct for you and your immediate family.

I have a maxim I use when people tell me I am wrong about some direction I have chosen for my life: *"Do not judge me by your own expectations."* Hold that maxim in your mind but do not take forever to make up your mind. Remember another maxim: *"He who hesitates is lost."*

CRUORUORUORUD

Chapter 7
MEDICAL EXPENSES

In the workers' compensation system, there are five types of medical expenses that are subject to dispute.

1. Those that have been approved by the Board or are for approved sites but not yet paid or even billed.
2. Those that are for sites of injury or for treatment, medication, and/or appliances[36] still under dispute .
3. Those expenses that may come in the future for anticipated treatment.
4. Those expenses that may come in the future for **un**expected treatment.
5. Those paid by some private health insurance carriers (union, employer, spouse, etc.) or Medicare.

For the purpose of this chapter, I'm going to use the following example of a claimant with multiple injuries:

The claimant falls and claims to have injured their foot, hip, and neck.

1. The case is established for the foot.
2. The injury to the neck is disallowed.
3. And the injury to the hip is still in the process of being resolved.

Medical bills are relatively easy to deal with if you have a different doctor for each site of injury but most injured workers do not. A separate doctor does not make sense nor is it practical. But it does get complicated when you go to the same doctor for treatment to all three sites of injury. In the normal course of events, the carrier is responsible for all expenses related to the foot, none for the neck, and until the hip issue is resolved, none of the doctors get paid for the hip but still must treat the hip as if they were getting paid for that treatment. Some carriers will pay for the hip and neck if is a small portion of the overall expenses on a bill for treatment to the foot, when that bill is submitted by the doctor; this does

---

36... 'Appliances' refers in workers compensation terms to crutches, prosthetic limbs, eyeglasses, wheelchairs, TENS units, special beds, Whirlpool baths, specially equipped motor vehicles, false teeth, etc.

not necessarily mean that they have accepted the hip or neck as work-related site of injury. If there is a substantial bill (and one man's substantial is another man's *'not so big'*), the carrier may pay only for that part of the bill for which the injury has been formally established.

The vast majority of §32's state something to the effect that

> The carrier/Self-insured agrees to audit and pay for all medical bills, subject to medical arbitration and the New York Workers' Compensation Fee Schedule, for treatment of established, causally related sites of injury rendered prior to the approval date of this agreement. Payment of all other medical bills shall not be the responsibility of the carrier/Self-insured. The carrier/Self-insured also agrees to withdraw all C-8.1 objections upon approval of this settlement agreement[37]. The claimant also stipulates that there is no further claim for additional medical treatment, transportation, or miscellaneous expenses arising from this accident. The claimant further agrees that any need for medical treatment which may arise subsequent to the approval of this agreement will be the claimant's responsibility solely and not the responsibility of the employer and/or its workers' compensation carrier/Self-insured.

It is important to understand that once the case is settled,

1. The responsibility for paying for all medical treatment for sites of injury that have been allowed/established as part of the claim, i.e., the foot, have been transferred to the claimant. Part of the settlement included a sum of money the carrier had set aside, when the carrier was responsible for the claim, to pay for treatment to the foot. Now that the claimant has that money, the claimant must use it to pay the bills.

2. The claimant's private health insurance is responsible for sites of injury that the Board has determined were not as a result of the injury, i.e., the neck.

37...The C-8.1 forms are forms designed by the Board for use by carriers when they object to a any part of a medical bill.

3. And then there is the <u>hip</u>! This leads to two separate but somewhat related questions:
   (1) Who pays the bills for treatment before the settlement?
   (2) Who pays the bills for treatment after the settlement?

Leaving the unresolved site of injury, i.e., the hip, out of the agreement will lead to disputes not only with the workers' compensation carrier when bills for that site are received by them but the claimant's private health insurance and Medicare will also dispute their responsibility to pay for the medical treatment for the hip in the past or in the future.

The resolution is simple, subject of course to negotiations between the claimant and the carrier:

(1) The agreement can state that the carrier will pay for unresolved sites of injury, i.e., the hip (and these should be listed in the agreement) without taking any responsibility for them. But this does not resolve who will pay for future expenses.

(2) The agreement can state that the previously unresolved sites of injury, i.e., the hip, are accepted and being established as a part of the claim. Thus the carrier will pay for any prior bills for medical treatment to that site but the claimant then becomes personally responsible for any future treatment to that site, i.e., the hip, just as they are for the foot as the foot and hip will most likely NOT be covered by the claimant's personal/union/ family health insurance.

(3) The agreement can state that the previously unresolved sites of injury, i.e., the hip, are disallowed but that the carrier will pay for any prior bills for medical treatment to that site.

(4) The agreement can state that the previously unresolved sites of injury, i.e., the hip, is disallowed and the carrier is not responsible for paying for any prior bills for medical treatment to that site.

It was my practice that if I found either in the agreement or in the claimant's file that there were unresolved or alleged sites of injury, I would ask at the hearing that the agreement add language explaining how these would be resolved: who will pay for the pre-settlement bills and who would pay for the post-settlement bills for these sites.

◆Established Sites of Injury

These are bills for treatment to sites of injury, i.e., the foot, that have been approved by the Board but not yet paid or even billed.

The carrier by law must pay for these expenses once the claim has been established and the specific sites of injury have been established. In this case, so far only for the foot, the issues regarding the bills for this treatment are between the carrier and the medical provider. Just as if the case were to stay open, any disputes between the medical provider and the carrier as to the cost incurred before the date of settlement are between the carrier and the medical provider:

- treatment
- the frequency of the treatment
- medications
- appliances
- or even if the treatment is proper

The Board has a procedure to resolve these disputes, which is covered by NYCRR §325.6. The claimant is NOT responsible for any bills that the carrier does not pay that fall under this category. If a medical provider sends the claimant a bill or has a collection agent call the claimant, the claimant should contact his attorney; even if the case had been settled and the attorney paid, the attorney still works for the claimant on any matters relating to the claim. If the claimant does not have an attorney (the claimant is 'pro-se', i.e., for themselves), contact the Board's Advocate for Injured Workers at 800-580-6665, 20 Park Street, Albany, NY 12207. If this happens more than once, I suggest the claimant have a copy of the following text handy to read or write back to whomever is demanding payment.

Please note that this bill covers treatment related to my established workers' compensation claim for which all medical expenses are the responsibility of the workers' compensation carrier. Under the New York State Workers' Compensation Law, not only do I have no legal responsibility to pay for these bills but you are not allowed to hold me responsible for them. You must contact the insurance carrier or the Workers' Compensation Board's Bureau of Health Management - Office of Health Provider Administration at (800) 781-2362.

◆Alleged Sites of Injury

These are bills that are for sites of injury still under dispute, i.e., the hip, for which payment is pending the Board's decision if the site of injury is work-related or not. If they are determined to be work-related, the carrier pays; if not, the claimant's private insurer pays; and if the claimant has no private health insurance, the claimant is personally responsible.

These unresolved sites of injury are subject to negotiation and should be clearly spelled out in the agreement. I always felt that it was best when the disputed sites of injury were listed in the agreement and then the specific reference made to them when dealing with medical bills.

Also it would be helpful to the claimant if the unresolved sites of injury were specifically either '*allowed*', i.e., considered a part of the injury, or '*disallowed*', specifically not a part of the injury.

This covers two separate but somewhat related options and a third option combing the two:

Option 1: The carrier agrees to pay for sites of injury still not settled: This means that the carrier has agreed that (1) the sites of injury not previously resolved, i.e., the hip, were in fact injured as a result of the accident and (2) the carrier will pay for all expenses related to the treatment of the injury through the date of the settlement. But this also means that any future treatment is the responsibility of the claimant.

Option 2: The carrier agrees to be responsible for all bills for medical treatment received to date for the disputed site, i.e., hip, without accepting that this injury is an established site of injury in this claim. This means that the carrier will pay for these expenses up through the date of the hearing.

Option 3: The carrier agrees that it will not be responsible for any medical bills for the treatment of the disputed site of injury, i.e., the hip. Payment for these then become the responsibility of the claimant's private health insurer or the claimant.

Or some mix of the first two, But specificity is the key so that when a medical bill arrives at the claimant's door in two, three, or six months, it is clear whether or not the claimant is responsible for it.

The carrier can deal with late submission of bills under NYCRR §325-1.24(b). But medical bills for disallowed sites as well as unestablished sites (unless covered in the §32) are the sole responsibility of the claimant. And even if the claimant has health insurance that would pay for bills for sites not covered by the §32, most private health insurers have time limits for receiving bills. It is likely that if there was a law suit by the claimant's medical provider, or more likely the provider's collection agency, the claimant would win. But to put it bluntly, "*Who needs the hassle*?" An experienced workers' compensation attorney or licensed rep will make sure that this issue of old-but-not-yet-submitted medical bills is covered one way or the other so that the claimant does not have to deal with this problem once the agreement is done and the case is closed.

◆Expenses for expected future medical treatment

In virtually all settlements, it will be the claimant's responsibility to pay all the bills the claimants get for the treatment after the settlement is approved, those very same expenses which, until the date of the agreement, had been paid for by the carrier.

The State of New York has a medical fee schedule that covers every procedure that the claimant can think of, with a specific dollar value attached to it. So whether the claimant's medical provider puts $1000, $100, or $10 down in the bill, the medical provider will be paid by the carrier the amount on the medical fee schedules or the actual bill, whichever is less.

The claimant, on the other hand, will be treated differently. The claimant's medical provider, pharmacy, etc. can charge the claimant what they want: more, less, the same, or anything in between. If the claimant is getting regular treatment from a medical provider, it is recommended that the claimant contact the provider BEFORE entering into the agreement and find out what the medical provider will charge. Since the amount the medical provider charges the carrier is already in the claimant's files (usually on the Form C-4 as shown on page 134 in Appendix F), the claimant can compare what the medical provider says he will charge the claimant with what that medical provider has been charging the carrier.

The carrier, who has been paying the claimant's bills in the past and has undoubtedly had thousands of other claimants who had the same injuries and treatments as the claimant, has a very accurate estimate of what will be the carrier's future medical costs. Therefore, the carrier will have included that amount when it calculates the settlement, although the carrier will not give the claimant that confidential information. That is, unless the claimant requires a Medicare set-aside but more on that later, a complex issue for which the entire Chapter 13 - *Medicare & Set Asides* starting on page 98 is dedicated. The '*set-aside*' is the amount that the carrier has determined will be the future medical costs for the claimant's injury, specifying that amount in the agreement, and assuming/suggesting that the claimant '*set this aside*' in a special account for use only to pay the relevant medical bills.

But, once the agreement is approved, it becomes the claimant's responsibility to pay for these expenses.

And for this I have a suggestion.

During all of my hearings, I was amazed how often, when I asked the claimant if they knew what their medical expenses would be in the future or even how much were the bills in the past that were paid for by the carrier, the answer was, "*I do not know.*" Since the claimant will be responsible for paying the claimant's future medical bills, and the amount of those bills will use up some of the money in the settlement which the claimant may have expected to use for income, it only makes sense that the claimant would want to know the claimant's possible financial risks in the future.

I suggest that if the claimant is getting regular medical treatment, the claimant check with the claimant's medical provider to see how much the provider will bill the claimant in the future. But if the claimant's future bills are more or are less than either the carrier estimated and/or the claimant guessed, that is either the claimant's gain or loss. No going back to the carrier for a redo!

◆Expenses for <u>un</u>expected future medical treatment

Sometimes, as the result of a work-related injury, something unexpected happens. The claimant can have a bad foot and for years everything has been fine. But one day, while going up the stairs, the foot gives out, the claimant falls and has a new injury, i.e., the claimant's knee. If the claimant's case were still open, the claimant could ask to have this new injury considered as being 'consequential'[38] to the claimant's initial injures and seek additional compensation, if as a result of this consequential injury, the claimant's disability has changed. And the claimant could get the carrier to pay for relevant medical care for the claimant's knee.

But once the claimant takes the settlement, the possible risk of consequential injuries is transferred from the carrier to the claimant. While it is true that these occurrences are rare, they do happen.

There was a case which got a bit of publicity a few years ago which dealt with a claim for an injury to the claimant's leg while he was doing clean-up at the World Trade Center in 2001. The claimant took a §32 settlement a few months later which closed his case forever. Two years later, he developed a serious lung condition as a result of his alleged exposure at the clean up in 2001 but he could not collect anything from the workers' compensation carrier because, a few months before he was diagnosed with lung problems, he had settled his claim for any and all injuries and medical conditions condition relating to that date, even if at the time of the settlement he did not know all the future possible medical complications that could arise. That is how all the agreements are drafted so there is always the risk of some future consequential injury, a risk, albeit small, the claimant must factor into their decision.

38...'Consequential' and 'causally-related' injuries are more fully defined in Chapter 14 - _Frequently Asked Questions_, on page 106

◆What about my personal health insurance, employer/union health plan, or Medicare/Medicaid?

The claimant must understand that the basic concept of workers' compensation insurance is that the claimant's employer, through his insurance, is responsible for all medical treatment that the claimant needs for these work-related injuries, basically for the rest of the claimant's life. They are not supposed to give the claimant a few thousand dollars to '*get lost*' and then have some other entity pay for the claimant's expenses.

The claimant has the responsibility of telling anyone else that the claimant goes to for medical treatment that the claimant got injured at work. Not only must the claimant tell them this when seeking treatment after having settled their case with a §32, the claimant must also inform the medical provider before the case is settled. Most insurance forms and doctors' questionnaires ask the question: "*Did this injury happen at work?*" To lie about prior workers' compensation injuries can result in some serious problems for the claimant. And, yes, I am sure that the claimant has a buddy who has been lying for years, but that does not mean that the claimant will not be the poor schnook[39] who gets his name in the newspaper after having been alleged to have committed insurance fraud. In addition, the claimant can lose his insurance policy for having committed fraud by lying, and could jeopardize someone else's policy if the claimant is on theirs, i.e., spouse or parents.

<u>Medicare payment</u> for workers' compensation injuries is a very complex legal matter. Medicare will pay for expenses related to injuries the claimant received while working but only after several very stringent conditions have been met which include the claimant using a predetermined amount of the claimant's settlement (the Medicare set-aside) to pay for those expenses. As a result the entire Chapter 13 - <u>*Medicare & Set Asides*</u>, starting on page 98, is devoted to this subject.

<u>Private health insurance</u>: Private health insurance usually does not

---

39... A Yiddish term for the one guy in a group of 100 all of whom violate the laws but is the only one who gets caught.

cover pre-existing conditions[40] and virtually none will cover work-related injuries. In fact, if the claimant placed a claim with his private health carrier when the claimant first got injured and that private carrier discovered that the claimant had placed a claim for workers' compensation, the private carrier would not pay any future bills until the case has been resolved at which time they would send copies of the bills they did pay to the claimant's workers' compensation carrierand tell them, *"Hey, we paid these but if it's a worker's compensation case, you have to reimburse us."*

While the private carrier will get reimbursed, it will be according to the NYS workers' compensation fee schedule, not necessarily what the claimant's private carrier would have paid or did pay the claimant's doctor. Any difference is the private carrier's problem, not the claimant's. But if the claimant tries to '*fool*' them, the claimant could end up losing his coverage and '*his coverage*' can mean in whose ever's name the policy is so that if the claimant is included in their spouse's policy, the spouse (and children) could lose their policy coverage, too.

Again, when I point out the downside, the odds of it happening to the claimant may be small. But would **you** want to be the poor schnook whose name is in some insurance industry press release?

Employer/unions health plans: Employer/unions health plans sometimes are written with language that allows/requires them to cover ALL medical expenses to the extent that, while the claimant has an open workers' compensation claim, they will not pay, but once the claim is closed, even if the claimant got a settlement which included some money for future medical expenses, the employer/union plan will pay. But the claimant should check with the manager of the plan in advance of finalizing the agreement.. The interpretation of health plans can be very complex and there was a major federal case[41] a few years ago which essentially said that, once the claimant takes a §32, the claimant automatically removes himself from the employer's health plan for any medical costs

---

40...Under the new federal laws, known as Obama-care, laws as to whether a carrier must cover pre-existing conditions has changed but whether this will apply to workers compensation injuries when a case has been settled has not been raised..

41...Dorato v Blue Cross of Western NY US District Court, W.D. NY, 163 F.Supp

associated with that workplace injury or any medical problems that develop as a consequence of that injury.

◆Medicare

Medicare, the federal government program that pays for medical treatment to those who are retired and/or disabled, is, by law, not supposed to pay for medical treatment for any work related conditions. There are some conditions under which it will pay but these are very strict, complex, and ever-changing.

Chapter 7 - _Medicare & Set-Asides_ (page 98) gives a brief explanation, very brief and very simplistic. There are dozens of websites, books, magazine articles, and research papers as well as training seminars to explain to workers' compensation attorneys all over the country how Medicare interacts with workers' compensation settlements. As to how it relates to the individual claimant's case, I suggest the claimant speak to his workers' compensation attorney.

◆Summary

Earlier in this chapter, I suggested that the claimant speak to his medical provider in order for the claimant to find out how much it is going to cost the claimant in the future for the medical treatment for which the claimant's workers' compensation carrier has been responsible in the past. The claimant should also check with his medical provider to make sure that any invoices for services provided before the date of the claimant's settlement have been sent to the carrier. The reason for this is that some doctors use outside companies to handle their billing, and they may be two, three, four, or more months behind in processing bills. The claimant does not want to be in the unfortunate situation of having a bill arrive in the amount of $500 or $1000 which nobody knew about. If it is for a site of injury, i.e., foot, accepted as a part of the claim, the carrier is responsible no matter how late after treatment the bill arrives; actually if the bill arrives very late, the carrier may not have to pay it and, if this happens, the medical provider can not come after the claimant.

In most cases, a properly prepared §32 agreement will cover these late bills. But the more preparation that is done in advance of closing the claimant's case, the fewer problems the claimant will have in the future. This could be considered similar to finding a charge on the claimant's credit card bill for something that the claimant did not buy. While there will be no problem getting the charge removed from the claimant's bill, the claimant does not need to waste time or have the stress of dealing with the problem.

An open workers' compensation claim means that the carrier is responsible for the claimant's future treatment as it relates not only to the claimant's original injury but to any future/consequential medical problems that can occur which the Board determines is a *'consequential'* or *'causally related'* medical condition. But once the claimant signs off on a §32 settlement, the responsibility for past medical bills depends on the status of the claimant's injuries and the terms of the claimant's agreement. BUT all future medical expenses become the claimant's sole responsibility.

CR8OCR8OCR8OCR8O

Chapter 8
AGREEMENTS EXCLUDING MEDICAL

In some cases, it may be in the claimant's best interest not to settle the case if there is a concern about high ongoing or possible future medical expenses. Therefore, although the claimant may be willing to take the financial risk regarding possible future lost wages by closing the case, the claimant is unwilling to take the risk and worry about what happens if the medical expenses are much higher than calculated at the time of the settlement.

There is a way to settlement the claim, however:

a compensation only settlement

In these types of settlements, the claimant waives all right to future compensation just as is done in the much more common §32 agreement but no money is included that would otherwise have represented the carrier's payment of future medical expenses, anticipated or not. These settlements are similar but not quite the same as the Lump Sum Settlements covered in Chapter 2 - _Settlements Prior to §32's_ starting on page 12. The key difference is that lump sum settlements can on occasion be reopened whereas the §32 settlement means the case can never be reopened.

These '_non-medical_' agreements state that the cost of any medical treatment and issues relating to frequency and type of treatment remain open, with all disputes to be resolved by the Board, just as they had been before the settlement was offered. Just as in cases that have never been closed, the claimant is free to move out of New York, as the workers' compensation law does go into detail as to the responsibilities that the carriers have for paying for medical treatment received out of state. However, if you still live in New York, whether or not the claimant's entire case or just the claimant's medical is open, does not mean you can go out-of-state for treatment; you can under some circumstances but it is always appropriate to check with your attorney or the Board before you do so.

As a result, the claimant, from a personal income perspective, is no longer under the eye of the carrier. Whether or not the claimant works (and if not working, why not), and how much the claimant is earning is no longer of any interest to the carrier and thus no longer a potential area of fights between the claimant and the carrier.

There is usually only one issue left to be resolved: the agreement.

Normally at this point in time in the case, all sites of injury have been established and other sites raised at the beginning of the case not established have been disallowed, although there is the possibility that there may be one site whose status is not yet resolved, that hip again.

◆Options

The agreement should state one of the following

Option 1: No additional sites of injury, 'consequential' or 'causally related' can be added to this claim for purposes of the carrier having any responsibility to pay for treatment to these new sites.

Option 2: The claimant does not waive the right to have additional sites of injures included in the claim, be they 'causally related' or 'consequential' but the resolution of any controverted issues as to whether or not a 'new' or 'consequential' site shall be considered a part of this claim shall remain within the jurisdiction of the Board.

Option three: If no additional sites of injury can be added to the claim, if there are any unresolved sites of injury, i.e., the hip, the agreement must state that site will be established or disallowed.

Carriers for the most part do not like these agreements. While regular §32 agreements include money for compensation and medical, these 'no-medical' settlements are for compensation only. The result is that the amount of money offered for the compensation may be less, an incentive for the claimant to take a full §32 settlement.

In settlements of this nature, any issues relating to Medicare or private health insurance are irrelevant because the carrier to whom the responsibility for the claim was assigned will still have that same responsibility for all future medical claims subject to the limitations noted in one of the three options listed above.

CR80CR80CR80CR80

Chapter 9
§32 LEGAL FEES

All attorneys charge legal fees so, unless the claimant is *pro-se* (see page 33), the claimant will have to pay a legal fee. In workers' compensation, legal fees are paid on the awards made for compensation but not on any medical bills associated with the claim, even if the medical bills and/or treatment are subject to a dispute.

◆What is the law on fees?

While Workers' Compensation Law references the legality of fees (§24 and NYCRR 300.17 in regular decisions and 300.36(h) for §32's), the law actually says very little else about fees. The only reference to the amount of a fee is §300.17(d)(1) which states that if the attorney or licensed rep is seeking a fee equal to or in excess of $450, the attorney or licensed rep must file an OC-400.1 form which is, in effect, a blank invoice for a legal fee. But neither that form nor any language in the law dictates what must be listed in terms of services performed. The Board's rules simply state that *"an agreement may provide for reasonable fees commensurate with the services rendered by the claimant's attorney or licensed representative."* The phrase *"worked for claimant"* has been accepted by some law judges and commissioners as a sufficient explanation. Essentially, the amount of the fee is dictated by precedent.

◆From whose money is the fee paid?

The fee is taken out of awards made to the claimant. No awards - no fees. Thus if the case is not for lost wages but only for medical treatment, the attorney is likely to get no fee. The judge may award a fee but it is as *'debt'* that will not be paid to that attorney until such time as awards are made to the claimant. And, if no more money is awarded in the future for lost time, then the attorney just does not collect the fees that were awarded to him.

◆Who writes out the check for the fee?

Under the New York State Workers' Compensation Law, claimants are not permitted to pay any money directly to their attorney nor may the attorney ask for or accept any money from the claimant. All fees at all stages of a workers' compensation claim are paid to the attorney with the checks written out by the carrier and, then, only after they have been approved by a Board's law judge or commissioner.

If it is an ongoing case, the law judge determines the amount of the fee and how it is to be paid. He must determine if the fee is to be:

1. deducted from a large payment made to the claimant for prior awards not yet paid, referred to as *'money moving'*,[42]

2. withheld from the weekly compensation payments made to the claimant and held by the carrier until it totals $75-$100 at which time the carrier then sends that portion of the fee to the attorney,

or

3. partially paid out of money moving and the balance on a weekly basis.

◆What is a fair fee?

As was noted in Chapter 2 <u>Settlements Prior to §32's</u> starting on page 17 in the analysis of fees awarded on this predecessor of the §32, fees for lump sum settlements were usually 10% except in the very rare cases where the claimant had not yet been classified. But the 15% was rare because the claimants had to be classified to quality for the lump sum (§15-b) settlement.

When §32's were first drafted, the attorneys used the same fee formula: 10% for claimants that had been classified and 15% for those who were not classified. And there was no $100 added as was often done in New York City for the §15-5b Lump Sum Settlements: there was no longer any requirement that the claimants had to undergo a medical examination by a Board doctor at the Board office the day of the hearing. In addition, most commissioners were starting to deduct that $100 from the legal fees in the §15-5b settlement.

For many years, with few exceptions, this was the accepted fee structure: unwritten in both the Workers' Compensation Law and the rules and regulations but written into the agreements by the claimants' attorneys and accepted by the commissioners who heard the cases.

42...'*Money moving*' means the net amount of money moving to the claimant, the amount on the check. This may be after legal fees or after adjustment for over-payment or under-payments of prior awards or compensation rates..This is further explained on page 112

Yes, there were a few occasions when the quality of representation of an attorney for a claimant seeking a §32 was below what was acceptable and a few commissioners did cut the customary fee. But, with rare exception, all fees were awarded as requested in the agreement.

◆If the claimant thinks the fee is unfair?

There are occasions when the claimant, although he has signed the agreement with the fee clearly written out, feels that he has done so under duress. And when asked by the commissioners or, since 2007, by the law judge if he agrees with the fee, answers '*No!*'[43]

And it is certainly the claimant's right to do so. The claimant can even proceed with a settlement even if the claimant's attorney does not think that it is in the claimant's best interest. But even then the attorney can still earn the fee. And the commissioners and law judges will listen to the attorney's explanation of why the agreement is not in the claimant's best interest and, on occasion, will agree and reject the settlement.

In these cases, the person conducting the hearing will ask the claimant to explain why the amount of the fee is unfair and then the attorney has the opportunity to justify the fee.

After all their presentations are made, the commissioner/law judge conducting the hearing makes a decision. The claimant's attorney has no say in the final decision, although the attorney is free to voice an opinion and usually does. But if the claimant does not like the fee set by the commissioner/law judge, they do have the right to not accept the settlement. And their attorney does have the right to make an appeal to a panel of three commissioners about the fee reduction but not otherwise stop the settlement from proceeding. In the event the claimant's attorney appeals, the disputed fee amount is withheld by the carrier until the Board panel makes its decision. If not all the money being withheld by the carrier is paid awarded to the claimant's attorney as a fee, the balance is then sent to the claimant.

The commissioner/law judge will not allow a claimant to cut the attorney

---

43...The fact that this question, "*Is the legal fee OK?*" is also on a Board supplied form which is usually completed with the assistance of the claimant's attorney and then handed in before the hearing is set does not mean that it reflects the claimant's thoughts on the issue. Page 116 in Appendix A *§32 Waiver Questions*

out of the process just so that the claimant can keep all of the settlement.

◆Can an attorney not in the agreement ask for a fee?

Yes. These requests happen under two conditions:

Prior attorney seeks a fee

The claimant had at least one attorney represent him prior to the attorney who is now representing him on the §32 being settled. That prior attorney feels that he has done work for the claimant in the past but has not yet received a proper fee for that work. As a result, the prior attorney will make a request at the hearing (he must appear in person). Next, the claimant makes a statement as to whether or not that prior attorney should receive a fee, and finally the current attorney makes a statement. Sometimes the commissioner/law judge will ask the two attorneys to step outside for a few minutes and attempt to resolve the issue. If the attorneys and claimant cannot come to an agreement between themselves, the commissioner/law judge will make the final decision. But the result is that the fee written into the agreement is not increased; it is divided between the attorneys.

Current attorney is left out of agreement

Sometimes, a carrier will contact the claimant directly offering a §32 settlement, suggesting but not stating directly that the claimant will save money by not having an attorney. The New York State Bar Association has a rule which strictly prohibits an attorney directly contacting the other party in a legal action if that other party has an attorney. Thus it is usually the case that it is examiners for the carrier who will make that phone call offer, equally unethical but not specifically prohibited by the Bar Association or the Board.

In some cases, it is the claimant who calls the carrier directly, after turning down an offer negotiated earlier by the attorney, figuring he can save on the attorney's fee, noted in page 33 in Chapter 4 - *Do You Need An Attorney?*

The claimant's '*prior*' attorney (the attorney he just tried to by-pass) will get a notice that the settlement hearing has been set, a notice sent by the Board. The claimant's attorney will show up, fee request in hand, if not previously submitted to the Board. As noted in the prior section, all parties will be given the opportunity to argue about the fee. The commissioner/law judge will then make a decision, with the fee to be deducted from the amount of the settlement offer. As previously noted, the commissioner/law judge will not allow a claimant to cut the attorney out of the process just so that the claimant can keep all of the settlement.

The chance of the carrier offering more money to pay the fee in order to settle the case is between '*zero and none*'.

In both cases, if the claimant does not like the commissioner/law judge's decision as to the amount of the fee, the claimant can refuse to accept the §32 agreement.

◆Law judges and legal fees

When §32's first started to come before the Board and the commissioners, the Office of the General Counsel determined that since the claimant's attorney was not a '*party of interest*' but just an '*interested party*'[44] the claimant's attorney had no right to appeal the fee if it was reduced by the commissioner/law judge at the hearing or simply denied in its entirety. But that changed when the hearings were transferred to the law judges.

In one particular district office, Manhattan, a few of the law judges, for reasons never made clear, determined that the claimants' attorneys were being overpaid for their work and started to reduce fees by as much as 90%.

When the attorneys first complained, they were told that since they were not a '*Party of Interest*', there was nothing they could. But what started to happen was that attorneys did not want their settlements heard in Manhattan but in Brooklyn or Queens, interfering with scheduling in Brooklyn and Queens (the other two NYC district offices) and many complaints were being heard at the Board's executive offices. Afer all, the attorneys did represent the claimants not only in the settlement

---

44...Both these terms are defined in Chapter 12 - *Who Participates in the Agreement?* on page 92

discussions but also for extended periods of time without a fee, waiting for awards to be made, from which the fees could then be paid.

The Office of the General Counsel reviewed the issue and then reversed its earlier decision and allowed the attorneys to appeal, an appeal heard by a panel of three commissioners. A quick review showed that three judges, all in Manhattan, one of whom had just retired, out of 69 statewide, accounted 25% of the appeals. The commissioners heard these appeals, made the appropriate adjustments, and this issue slowly died out, although there still are some law judges who still feel they have not only the right but the obligation to award minimal fees to claimant's attorneys..

◆Summary

The claimant's attorney, as much as he may like you and want to fight for the rights of injured workers, does not run a charity. Claimants' attorneys run a law practice and, in addition to making a living practicing law, also have the expenses of running a business: rent, phone and other utilities, staff, office equipment and all the other costs necessary to maintain an effective legal service, all of which are to the benefit of the injured worker.

The current fee structure has served not only the attorneys but also the injured workers by making sure that there are qualified professionals out there who can help them get proper compensation and medical treatment after they are injured at work.

CA80CA80CA80CA80

Chapter 10
HEARINGS

As of the date that this book has been written, claimants wishing to settle their claim by a §32 agreement must appear before a law judge. And it is sometimes at these hearings that the issue comes up as to whether or not this is a *'fair'* settlement. In reality, the determination of whether or not an agreement is *'fair'* at the hearing is usually one that means the agreement is *'fair'* to the administrative law judge. As to whether or not it is *'fair'* to the claimant in terms of money and medical, that is the subject of Chapter 6 - <u>What is a good value</u>, which starts on page 50.

Under the Board's original interpretation of the law and the rules and regulations that permitted §32 agreements, claimants had to appear in person in front of a commissioner in order to settle the §32. Then on September 1, 2000 the Board decided to process §32 waiver agreements differently. To speed up the handling of §32 settlements and to save the commissioners the need to attend hearings, the Board made a decision that many §32 settlements could be done administratively. This meant that the agreement could go to a commissioner who just reviewed the papers and approve it without ever asking the claimant if he knew what he were doing and what the agreement meant, both now and in the future.

Then, in an April 2004 legal decision issued by the New York State Appellate Court, Third Department (the matter of <u>Hart v. Pageprint/DeKalb,</u> 6 A.D.3d 947' 775 N.Y.S.2d 195;2994 N.T. App.Div. LEXIS 4784, April 22, 2004), the Board was told that the Board has to restructure the way that they had been doing the administrative decisions and hold hearings or formally change the rules and regulations. For a number of reasons, many of which involved internal Board politics and personalities, it was decided that as of September 2007, there would be no more administrative decisions, the commissioners would be relieved of the responsibilities of doing the §32's, and all §32's would be heard by the administrative law judges, to be added to their already full regular workload.

Even though the commissioners as a group had participated in excess of 30,000 to 40,000 §32 settlement hearings, it was decided that the attorneys at the executive offices of the Board in Albany would be the ones who would set the procedures for the administrative law judge without any input of the commissioners.

When commissioners were conducting the §32 hearings, each commissioner would do anywhere between one and six days of hearings a month, each consisting of 8 to 15 cases. As a result, whether it took two hours or four hours to complete their calendar for the day, the commissioners did have the time to discuss at length, if necessary, any pending issues with the claimant. The law judges on the other hand have very strict *'production'* schedules and are given only a limited amount of time to handle each §32 settlement that comes before them.

As a result, when commissioners were doing the §32's, minor problems in the agreement and misunderstandings by the claimant could be resolved either at the hearing or a case could be adjourned for one week to give the parties time to work out the problems. My records show that the conscientious commissioners would adjourn approximately one out of every 20 cases that they had. The law judges on the other hand, because of their strict time schedule, felt that they had two options: either approve the §32 agreement or reject the §32 agreement.

Also, there were some law judges who felt that because they were sitting at the end of the table on a raised platform, they had some sort of superior intellectual and moral authority and would ask a lot of questions that the commissioners felt were not only not necessary but totally inappropriate.

A lot of these questions dealt with the personal financial status of the claimant. Some law judges (and a few commissioners) would reject the claim because, sitting on the raised platform, felt, as *'protectors'* of the injured worker, they knew what was in the best interest of the claimant who obviously (to the law judge/commissioner) would be unable to make a proper decision.

As I used to tell my colleagues and friends, the fact that a governor in his infinite wisdom nominated us to be a commissioner and the State Senate, in its own infinite wisdom, confirmed us, does not imbue any of us with any additional wisdom or insight. Some could say we are the same #%$'% we were before our confirmation but only now with a title. I, for one, could not disagree when I was on the Board nor now that I am not.

I do remember a case that came before me on appeal in which the law judge stated that the claimant did not understand what she was doing when she wanted to accept a §32 settlement because the claimant would not have enough money to live on. I raised a number of points to explain my reasoning why the law judge was in error.

The first point was that the very same claimant testified on a number of occasions before that same law judge in all her prior hearings; obviously she was competent enough for the law judge to have allowed her to testify all those years.

As to the second point, the question of having enough money to live on, it was this very same law judge who for years had refused to make a ruling on her rate of compensation so she got none. Yet, the claimant had managed to survive all those years on '*not enough*' money because that judge failed to make a decision on her rate of compensation. So much for the "*lack of competence and judgement*" on the part of the claimant.

I was at a total loss as to how this judge could question the competence of this woman and also determine that there was not enough money in the settlement for her. Whatever was the amount in the settlement, it was more than that same law judge ever awarded her to live on while her case was in front of him.

As to the financial status of a claimant, several commissioners found another reason this was not an appropriate question. §15-5b Lump Sum Settlements had a standard agreement, drafted by the Board, on which there were a number of questions about the claimant's financial status. Hence the answers to these questions were meant to be used when considering if the Lump Sum Settlement was fair. But these were not in the 1996 amendment to the workers' compensation law, there was no reference to a '*means test*.' Therefore, we did not see any legal justification for asking questions on this subject.

As an example of how unfair is this subjective "*I know what's best for you*" approach, consider a §32 settlement with which I was involved.

> The case had never been established; no decision was made as to whether or not the claimant would qualify for compensation and medical payments. Both parties decided to settle rather than taking the risk of winning or losing. The commissioner who was hearing the settlement decided that the amount of the settlement was too low and therefore unfair to the claimant and rejected the §32. The case itself then went before a law judge, a process which the parties had hoped to avoid, and the claimant won the case, entitling her to

benefits in excess of what was in the settlement rejected by that commissioner.

The carrier appealed the law judge's decision and the case went before a panel of three commissioners. The panel unanimously reversed the law judge and disallowed the claim, leaving the claimant with nothing. And who was on this panel? None other than the very same commissioner who originally rejected the §32 as offering the claimant too little money.

If the law judge is going to ask claimant detailed financial information as to how the claimant has decided whether the amount of the settlement is fair, then we should ask the carrier the financial basis for which it made its offer.

Asking the claimant to review all the claimant's other sources of income, the claimant's spouse's income, or whether or not they are married, living together with someone and sharing expenses are, in the opinion of many of my colleagues, an invasion of the claimant's privacy. Plus, as I have previously noted, the vast majority of these claimants have survived financially up to the date of the hearing. With rare exception, and these will not be uncovered by asking detailed financial questions of the claimant, the financial status of the claimant should not be relevant. And that information could, in some cases, result in the carrier withdrawing the offer.

I doubt a carrier would reveal those kind of details which would reveal confidential business information about methods of calculation of potential insurance losses, determinations which insurance companies use to help them set their premium rates and, in effect, stay in business. Even the New York State Insurance fund, the insurer of last resort, a quasi-pubic/private insurance carrier, uses the same methods of calculation to make a surplus/profit every year.

◆Pre-Hearing Coaching

It is at the hearing that the final decision is made. For many claimants this may be their first time in front of a law judge. Or perhaps, it is a law judge they have never met before. And when it was the commissioners who did the hearings, the attorney's would impress upon the claimants the fact that it was not '*just*' a law judge but a '*commissioner*' who would be hearing the case.

In any event, some claimants were nervous and had problems answering some of the questions. Of course this did not always occur because some commissioners and law judges don't ask any questions about the agreement itself. They ask the same 10 questions to everyone who comes into the hearing part. It is even possible that they did not even read the §32. They were just as anxious to get the hearing completed and go onto something more important to them.

But there are times when there are questions and the claimants do not want to risk getting the agreement rejected or the hearing postponed because they can not answer some basic questions. Hence the need for coaching.

However, if the claimants can not answer some of the basic questions, what are they doing getting a settlement in the first place? I have had claimants who could not tell me the amount of the settlement or their sites of injury. There was no justification for them being at a hearing, let alone even having a settlement.

A key point for the claimant to understand, as well as their attorneys, is that some of the questions require thoughtful responses. These are not questions that have a set answer, i.e. *"It was your right leg that was injured is that correct?"* or *"You are currently receiving $295.80 a week in compensation - is that correct?"*

The questions may be:

> Do you know what it will cost you for medical treatment in the future?

> Will you have enough one to live on? (A simple *'yes'* should suffice.)

> Do you understand you will have to pay for your own medical treatment in the future? (A simple *'yes'* should suffice.)

It is helpful if there is a sheet of paper in front of the claimant with a lot of basic information about the agreement. Not knowing the size of the settlement or the amount of the legal fee can raise a question as to whether the claimant knows what is going on. And if the claimant needs reading glass, he should bring them to the hearing and have them on.

As noted in Chapter 4 - _Do you need an attorney?_ on page 33, claimants' attorneys and licensed reps will coach claimants as to how to respond to the questions asked of them at the hearing by the commissioner, law judge, and sometimes even the carrier's attorney. It is as important to know what to say as it is to know what NOT to say.

◆Summary

If there is a law judge who decides they have been endowed with that unique moral and intellectual superiority which allows them to decide for the rest of the world what's fair (_'in their best interest'_) by asking a lot of inappropriate questions of the claimant, I suggest that before the claimant answer any such questions, the claimant whisper to their attorney, _"Now what?"_

Once, when I was being sued in a civil case, I was being questioned at a pre-trial hearing by the opposing attorney who kept pressing me to give him fast answers. I finally told him when he pushed me to give him a quick answer to a tricky question, _"Sorry, I am not like you - I have to think before I speak."_ You should do the same. It took you months, maybe even years, to get to the settlement hearing. A few more seconds or minutes will not make a difference.

But for the most part, the law judges just want to _'close'_ as many cases as possible and, more often than not, keep the §32 settlement hearing to the barest minium of time possible, while assuring that the claimant understands what is happening and that the settlement is not unfair.

CRUCRUCRUCRU

Chapter 11
IS THE MONEY ALL YOURS?

Yes, with a few exceptions, noted below.

◆Child support liens can be deducted

Under New York State's Workers' Compensation Law, money can be deducted directly from the settlement by the carrier if there is any lien for unpaid child support. This legal deduction is covered by WCL §33 *Assignments; exemptions*:

> Compensation . . . shall not be assigned, released or commuted . . . and shall be exempt from all claims of creditors and from levy, execution and attachment or other remedy for recovery or collection of a debt, [except] . . . shall be subject to application to an income execution or order for support enforcement pursuant to §5241 or §5242 of the civil practice law and rules.

In this case, the *'lien'* is the amount of child support that a New York State court has ruled that the claimant has not paid and, at the time of the settlement, remains unpaid. The State has the right to take that money from any cash the claimant may have or is about to collect, i.e., the §32 settlement. Normally, if small amounts are being deducted from whatever weekly awards the claimant has been getting, the carrier will already know about the lien, as will the Board.

To insure that it does not miss the opportunity to collect those past due child support liens, in September 1, 2006, the Board announced that it:

> entered into a data sharing agreement with the Division of Child Support Enforcement of the New York State Office of Temporary and Disability Assistance ('OTDA'), aimed at improving the collection of child support obligations from non-custodial parents. It has long been the policy of the Board that when a claimant owes a past-due child support obligation, the Board will not approve a Section 32 agreement involving that claimant unless the agreement provides that the support obligation will be paid in full out

of the settlement proceeds.

The Board will begin receiving a certified data file each month from OTDA, which will contain information on persons that owe past-due child support payable through a local district Support Collection Unit (SCU). Board examiners will check this data upon receiving a Section 32 agreement to determine if a claimant owes past-due child support. If past-due child support is owed, but is not addressed in the Section 32 agreement or the correct amount is not referenced, the examiner will notify the claimant that the Section 32 agreement will not be approved until the issue of the past-due child support is resolved. If a claimant disagrees with the information received from OTDA, he/she will need to contact the local district SCU to obtain a written statement with the correct information. If questions regarding child support arise, parties can contact the Division of Child Support Enforcement helpline at 1-888-208-4485.[45]

However, while some claimants may know that they have past due child support payments, they may not know that the past due amount MUST be deducted from the §32 settlement by the carrier. Unless they are made aware of the deduction and the exact amount (or very close to it), if the claimant only finds out about the lien after he gets his check and learns of the deduction, it is possible that the claimant can have the §32 ruled invalid. Therefore, it is in the claimant's best interest to make sure that his attorney know, certainly no later than the actual hearing, that the claimant has unpaid child support payments.

And this is not just limited to men, I did have one case in which the mother had close to $30,000 deducted from her settlement for past due child support.

There are some claimants who did not pay child support payments, not because they did not have the money, but because they objected to being held responsible for supporting their children. And it is obvious that, once they get their settlement which includes money representing future

---

45...Taken directly the the Board's website, under Subject Number 046-161.

compensation awards, they will not use any of the money from the settlement or whatever other income they may have to pay future child support.

The issue of future payments of child support has come up in every state in the United States which allows closing workers' compensation claims with a waiver agreement; some states make allowances for future payments and take that money out of a settlement while others do not. Until such time as the New York State Legislature decides to change the appropriate sections of the law, there is no way to make sure the claimant will use money from the settlement to pay future child support once the §32 settlement check has been paid.

◆Disability Claims & Liens can be deducted

While their workers' compensation claim was pending, some injured workers filed for disability benefits: payments made for time lost from work for non-work related injuries. If the claim is then established as a workers' compensation claim, the workers' compensation carrier and not the disability carrier is supposed to pay the claimant for that lost time. As a result, the disability carrier can seek to be reimbursed.

Title 12 NYCRR §363.12 provides that a disability carrier shall have a lien against an award of compensation. The disability carrier's interest in the workers' compensation claim arises from Disability Benefits Law (DBL) §206 and that interest consists solely of its right to assert a lien and claim reimbursement out of workers' compensation benefits. The disability carrier does not have a right to withhold consent to a §32 agreement, only the right to seek reimbursement. DBL §206(2) provides in relevant part:

> "If benefits have been paid under this article in respect to a disability alleged to have arisen out of and in the course of employment . . ., the employer or carrier . . . making such payment may, at anytime before award of workers' compensation benefits. . . is made, file with the Board a claim for reimbursement out of the proceeds of such award . . . and shall have a lien against the award for reimbursement . . . . ."

◆Taxes or credit card bills can not be deducted

If the claimant owes state, city, or federal taxes (income, real estate, etc), and there is a court order seeking payment, the Workers' Compensation Law §33 does not allow the carrier to withhold money from the settlement to pay those taxes, nor does it allow credit card companies or any other firms to whom the claimant may owe money to ask that carrier to withhold any money from the settlement.

Also, the settlements are usually free from city, state, or federal income tax. However, as noted earlier in this book, the tax laws are constantly changing and whether or not you have to show the settlement on your tax return, even if you do not pay taxes on it, or there is a tax on it, may well change in the coming years as city, state, and federal governments seek ways to balance their budget, even if it means unbalancing your own budget.

◆Third-party law suits

Under WCL §29, if the claimant has a law suit in civil court based on the accident that is the basis of the workers' compensation claim, the carrier does have the right to seek a certain level of reimbursement from the money that the claimant recovers. After all, if in the civil case the claimant wins $200,000 for medical expenses that have already been paid for by the workers' compensation carrier, it is only fair that the workers' compensation carrier be reimbursed.

The same holds true for any civil suit that results in money being awarded to the claimant for income lost as a result of the injury.

Third party settlements involve a great deal of complex law and there have been hundreds of cases that have gone to the New York State Appellate Courts and the Court of Appeals when carriers and claimants did not think that the Board's decisions were correct. If the claimant is involved in a third party lawsuit, has one pending, or just settled one, it is important to seek legal advice as to how this will affect not only the §32 settlement but any open workers' compensation case the claimant may have. And, as is often the case, an attorney specializing in workers' compensation law is far more knowledgeable on WCL §29 than an attorney who practices general law.

A note of warning: For those claimants who read this book and then decide to start a third-party law suit in order to get more money, it must be understood that the civil courts will only accept third-party law suits under very limited conditions. Any experienced workers' compensation attorney can explain why it is that 99.99% of workers' compensation claims can not also be taken to a civil court.

◆But ... after the check is deposited

However, once the claimant has deposited the settlement check into a bank account, those funds can be attached by a government agency or company, but only with a court order.

But lest the claimant be tempted to cash the settlement check at the bank or their local check cashing service rather than put it into a bank account of some sort, be forewarned: if someone sees the claimant taking a large amount of cash, follows the claimant home, and steals the money received from cashing the settlement check, then the claimant has nothing. And the claimant can not go back to the Board because he lost all the money.

The same holds true if the claimant invests it and loses it.

If the settlement has a 'medical set-aside', i.e., a specific amount noted for future medical expenses, page 98 in Chapter 13 - *Medicare & Set Asides* ,the claimant is in a better position depositing that money into a separate savings account and using that money for any medical expenses which he will incur in treating his work-related injury/disease for which the carrier would have paid if there were no settlement.

As noted in the *Chapter 13 - Medicare & Set Asides*, if the claimant wants to have Medicare pay for these work-related medical expenses after the §32 has been approved, one set of questions that Medicare will ask the claimant is *"What did you do with all the money from your settlement that was supposed to pay those expenses?"* By having a separate account and keeping track of all the expenses, the claimant will be able to answer Medicare quickly and not have an unnecessary delay in getting proper treatment or have the stress of fighting with the bureaucracy of the Social Security/Medicare system over who pays the bills.

◆Monthly Payments

In some cases, the claimant and carrier reach an agreement in which the money from the §32 settlement is put into a checking account owned by the claimant, an account on which the claimant can withdraw money on a periodic basis by writing a check. Many of these are done for those claimants who do not have checking accounts.

One advantage of this is that the claimant spends only an amount approximating the weekly compensation check he used to get from the carrier. It makes sure that the *'big amount'* of money in the account does not suddenly go for a trip, new home electronics, or a dozen other items previously out of financial reach of the claimant, their significant other, or their family and friends.

◆Annuity Accounts

In other cases, the funds from the settlement are put into an annuity account, which offers the many advantages noted above but offers guaranteed payments for a fixed period of time or even for life. Because the carrier is responsible for the money in the account, the Board has additional requirements:

> Section 32 agreements involving an annuity should expressly provide that the carrier will remain liable until all periodic payments have been made and will assume and continue the remaining periodic payments within thirty days of default by the company issuing the annuity.

> Section 32 agreements involving an annuity should contain a brief summary of the terms of the annuity, as follows: (a) the total amount payable pursuant to the annuity, (b) the cost (present value) of the annuity, (c) the schedule of payments to be made pursuant to the annuity and (d) what happens if claimant dies before all periodic payments are made.

> An annuity agreement need not be submitted to the Board or incorporated into the Section 32 agreement. If the

parties chose to do so, the Section 32 agreement should
also provide that insofar as the terms of the Section 32
Agreement and the annuity agreement conflict, the terms
of the Section 32 Agreement are controlling.

If any of these requirements are missing from the Section
32, the agreement should be returned indicating what is
required. A case note should be created indicating that the
agreement was returned for a guarantee, and/or the
inclusion of a brief summary, and/or a statement regarding
conflicting terms.

Certain aspects of annuity agreements can be quite complex and,
although these do help many claimants who settle their case with a §32
agreement manage their money, annuity agreements are NOT within the
jurisdiction of the New York State Workers' Compensation Board for
which reason I strongly suggest the counsel of an attorney or licensed
representative. For a sample of some of the complexities of annuity
agreements, you can read Appendix H - _Annuity Agreements_, starting on
page 137.

Remember that if the claimant is not working, these periodic withdrawals
from the checking account are to help cover living expenses, just as do
the weekly awards.

As previously noted, if the claimant spends the money all at once, it will
not be replaced.

◆Other investments

I am quite sure that all the claimant's friends and family will tell him how
to invest it: the stock market, gold, commodities, or a long shot at the race
track.

Well, unless they are calling the claimant from their 40-room mansion in
the Hamptons or their 60-foot yacht on Lake George, I would say that
whatever investment advice they are giving the claimant has either not
worked for them or perhaps they know better than to try these
suggestions with their own money.

There are a lot of large mutual funds (Vanguard, Fidelity, and Dreyfus, among others) and plenty of well-known brokerage firms whose investment advisers can help the claimant plan a CONSERVATIVE INVESTMENT.

As previously noted, if the claimant loses all the money from the settlement, it will not be replaced.

CBEOCBEOCBEOCBEO

Chapter 12
WHO PARTICIPATES
IN THE AGREEMENT?

By law, the compensation claim involves two distinct sets of participants:

The Parties of Interest
and
The Interested Parties

'*Parties of interest*' are the only ones who can sign the agreement whereas '*interested parties*' are those who have an interest in the agreement but no <u>legal</u> right to participate in it or set the terms of the settlement.

◆Parties of Interest

As used by the Board, the term '*Party of Interest*' refers to the claimant and the carrier(s). The agreement is between these two parties and only their signatures are required to make the agreement legal.

Occasionally, there is more than one carrier present.

UEF: Uninsured Employers Fund
This is a state- managed fund which steps in when the employer of the injured workers appears to have no insurance. The UEF participates in the process just like a carrier and has all the rights and responsibilities of any other carrier. If the UEF is ultimately found responsible for some or all of the expenses involved in the case, it can and will sue the employer, not only as a corporation but also the individual owners in order to get their money back. But for the claimant, the UEF is just another carrier. The UEF basically gets its money by charging all the workers' compensation carriers in New York a small fee on the premiums that they earn on the workers' compensation insurance that they sell.

Special Funds and Second Injury Fund
These are also funds created by state law. Depending on the age of the case and certain legal aspects of the case, these funds may share some of the financial responsibility with the carrier of record or take on all the financial responsibility. Like the UEF,

these funds get their money by charging all the workers' compensation carriers in New York a small fee. The Second Injury Fund is also known as the Special Disability Fund liability under both WCL §15(8) and a concurrent employment fund under WCL §14(6). As a result of changes in the 2007 amendments to the Workers' Compensation Law, these two funds are being closed, although for settlements of older cases, the funds may have some financial responsibility. This is not relevant to the claimant because the original carrier no longer has a potential '*partner*' to sharing the cost of the settlement.

Another Carrier

In some cases, particularly if there is more than one claim being settled, the cost of the claim and settlement may be apportioned between two private carriers.

Self-Insured Employer

Some employers, such as Verizon, have met certain financial standards set by the Board and the New York State Department of Insurance which allows then to be '*self-insured*' and participate in workers' compensation claims and settlements as if they were an actual carrier.

Self-Insured Group Trusts

These are groups of small and medium-sized employers who are too small individually to be '*self-insured*'. By getting together as a group, they pay their insurance premiums into the '*trust*' and as a group are then self-insured. The trusts are usually managed by '*trust management*' companies. These trusts participate in workers' compensation claims and settlements as if they were an actual carrier.[46]

New York City, counties, towns, and other government entities

Some of these political entities are self-insured, members of self-insured trusts, or represented by carriers.

Depending on the specifics of the case, more than one carrier's approval

---

46...In the last few years, there have been serious concerns about the financial stability of some of these trusts but, for the individual claimants, this makes no difference. If any trust, self-insured, or carrier, for that matter, is unable to meet its financial obligations, the State of New York will step in and take its place.

and signature may be required on the settlement, even if they are not
contributing any money toward the settlement.

Guardianships

Occasionally, there will be a claimant, who either because of the
injury they sustained or because of the medication that they are
taking, has difficulties understanding the agreement. As a result
the claimant may have a court-appointed guardian. Guardianships
are governed by Articles 17 and 17-A of the Surrogate's Court
Procedure Act (SCPA). Since the issue is a claimant with *'mental'*
issues, this situation is probably covered by Art. 17-A which deals
with *"mentally retarded or developmentally disabled persons"*.
However, there are other questions that need to be asked such as is
the claimant 18 or older and is this a *'limited'* guardianship. (See
SCPA §1756) The Board must to look at the court order granting
the guardianship as this should specify the powers of the guardian
in relation to the incompetent person's property. Hopefully, the
order includes the power to *"settle and compromise claims"*. More
often than not, such agreements and the guardianship papers are
submitted to the Board's Office of General Counsel for them to
confirm that the guardian has the authority to proceed on behalf of
the claimant.

◆Interested Parties

Board rules prevent any other parties from signing or participating in the
agreement even if they have some degree of interest in the settlement:
these are *'interested parties'*. Equally important, they have no legal
ability to prohibit the *'Parties of Interest'* from negotiating and signing
the §32 agreement.

Actually, statements to the effect that the agreement and/or any liens
therein have been approved by some other party (DB carrier, spouse,
medical provider, employer [unless it is the self-insured employer paying
for the settlement], third party carrier or defendant) are not allowed.

Claimant's attorney(s):

They are advisors to the claimants but, while it is recommended
that the claimants follow their advice, these attorneys are not
materially affected by decisions relating to the claim, other than
their fee. The New York State Appellate Court, Second

Department, in 2001, in the *Matter of Abel v. Wolff and Dungey, Inc. (287 A.D.2d 914 (2001), 732 N.Y.S.2d 118)* confirmed that the claimant's *"counsel had no legal standing to remain listed as a party to the agreement and the waiver could not be approved with a nonparty included therein."*

While the §32 agreement does have a signature line for the attorney or licensed representative to sign the agreement, their failure to sign the agreement does not change an otherwise valid agreement. The reason they sign is to prove that they were at the hearing to give advice to the claimant, even if the claimant rejected that advice.

Medical providers

Doctors, nurses, hospitals, ambulance services, pharmacies, etc., are part of the system because they provide necessary medical treatment. But the Board determines which treatments are necessary and how often treatment can be given as well as the fees to be paid the medical providers. If the medical providers have disputes on payment of the bills, the resolution of these issues does not involve the claimant. Hence, while they may have an interest in the outcome of the case or the settlement, they are not *'Parties of Interest.'*

Claimant's spouse and/or children

Obviously, they are directly affected by the outcome of the claim, and while they have a financial interest in the compensation and a personal interest in the physical recovery of the injured worker, they have no legal rights regarding the claim, unless there are child support liens. (See page 84 in Chapter 11 - *Is the money all yours?*.) Despite the fact that the claimant may not be able to personally finalize an agreement without their spouse's approval, the spouse's approval is not legally required.

The employer

Unless it is writing out the settlement check and is thus a *'Party of Interest'*, an employer is just an *'interested party'*.

When the employer buys the state-mandated workers' compensation insurance policy (unless it is self-insured), it automatically waives (gives up) its right to settle or negotiate an agreement. In fact, the employer waives its right to approve or fight against a claim and any of the rulings that take place during the life of the claim. In exchange for waiving its right to contest the claim and being a *'party of interest'*, the employer becomes an *'interested party'* while it is the carrier which takes on all of the financial responsibility for paying the compensation awards, medical bills and administrating the claim, including any legal expenses associated with fighting any part of the claim and/or negotiating the §32 settlement.

As a matter of law, these interested parties have no right to participate in regular hearings or the final §32 hearing. They may appear at a hearing but, since they are not a party of interest, they can not speak on any issues unless permitted to by the commissioner/law judge conducting the hearing.

I did have one case in which the claim had never been established. There was a question as to whether the injury was work related and, unless the claim was established, the carrier would not have to pay the medical provider the $20,000 billed by that medical provider; the bill would have to be paid for by the claimant's private health insurer if he had one or by the claimant directly, if he had the money (which he was getting under the settlement) and inclination to do so.

The §32 stated that the claim was disallowed, which relieved the carrier of paying the bill. Now, because the injuries were not work related, the claimant was responsible for the bills. The portion of the settlement that represented possible compensation was $40,000 and an additional $20,000 was included for medical bills. The medical provider, a chiropractor, had asked to speak to me before the hearing, stating that the claimant was planning to move out of the U.S. as soon as he got his $60,000 (less legal fee) and would most likely not use any of the $20,000 in the medical portion of the settlement to pay the doctor. Under the law, the doctor had no legal right to attach any of the money or require the carrier to withhold any money. It was obvious to me that it would be unfair to allow the claimant to get the $20,000 for his medical bills, leave the country, and leave the doctor with an uncollectible debt of $20,000. I told the claimant that this was unfair and suggested he, his attorney, the carrier's attorney, and the doctor take a few minutes before I would call the case for a hearing so that they could work out a solution. But, I added, there was no way I would let the claimant get the $20,000 for the medical and not be assured that the doctor would get paid. After a brief discussion, they agreed that the doctor would accept $7,000 and the carrier, with the claimant's approval, was to take $7,000 from the settlement and pay it directly to the doctor.

So while, in this case, the doctor was not a party of interest, it seemed that the only fair thing to do was to protect the interest of the doctor by making sure that the claimant paid him.

Essentially, while only the claimant and carrier can agree to and then sign an agreement, if the commissioner/law judge feels the agreement is unfair in any way, they will take the steps necessary to protect interested parties. The §32 agreement is to be for the benefit of the injured worker and the carrier but is not supposed to be used to place some other third party, an interested party, at a disadvantage.

CROCROCROCRO

Chapter 13
MEDICARE & SET-ASIDES

◆Medicare Set-Asides

The basic concept behind workers' compensation is that the employer for whom the claimant is working when injured is responsible, usually through a carrier, to pay for all the claimant's lost wages and medical expenses.

Ths means that the claimant's private/group/employer/union health insurance, federal Social Security or Disability, Medicare, or Medicaid is supposed to be responsible for those medical expenses.

As written in the Federal government's website dealing with this issue, all parties in a workers' compensation case have significant responsibilities under the Medicare Secondary Payer laws to protect Medicare's interests when resolving cases that include past and future medical expenses. The recommended method to protect Medicare's interests is a workers' compensation Medicare Set-aside Arrangement (WCMSA), which allocates a portion of the WC settlement for future medical expenses. The amount of the set aside is determined on a case-by-case basis.[47]

Therefore, like most other states, the New York State workers compensation system has various forms and procedures to insure that, if some other carrier has paid any of the expenses for the claimant's work related injury, it will be reimbursed for the moneys they paid out.

Workers compensation law also means that the injured worker and the carrier can not make an arrangement to shift the cost of any future medical expenses to these or any other other entities.

Since the vast majority of Americans will at one time or another retire and qualify for Medicare, the Federal Government has established a *'set aside'* program to insure that the interests of Medicare are protected, under the authority of Centers for Medicare & Medicaid Services, hereinafter referred to as CMS.

47...www.cms.gov/WorkersCompAgencyServices/02_workerscompensationoverv iew.asp

In order to protect its interest and make sure that future medical expenses are not shifted to it, CMS regularly issues various regulations which can be found under Title 42 Public Health and on its website[48]. In particular, 42 C.F.R. §411.46 and §411.47 state that workers compensation settlements must protect the interest of Medicare. And one way that this is done is for the agreement to *set aside* funds for future medical expenses.[49]

Because Medicare does not pay for workers compensation related medical services when an individual receives a workers compensation settlement that includes funds for future medical expenses, the claimant should consider Medicare's rules and regulation at the time of settlement. For this reason, CMS recommends that parties to a workers compensation settlement set aside funds in a specially designated account.

◆Medicare set aside disclosure form

As a step in this direction, there is an additional document titled Medicare Set Aside Disclosure Form, a copy of which is in Appendix K on page 143. Not only does this form explain the relationship between Medicare and the injured worker but the injured worker is required to sign it as a confirmation that he understands all the points raised in this Chapter.

◆Medicare Regulations

The Medicare website explains that:

> Pursuant to 42 U.S.C. §1395y(b)(2) and §1862(b)(2)(A)(ii) of the Social Security Act, Medicare is precluded from paying for a beneficiary's medical expenses when payment "has been made or can reasonably be expected to be made under a workers compensation plan, an automobile or liability insurance policy or plan (including a self-insured plan), or under no-fault insurance." Federal law (42 U.S.C. §1395y(b)) not only establishes that Medicare is a secondary payer to WORKERS COMPENSATION, but also that

---

48...www.cms.gov/WorkersCompAgencyServices/02_workerscompensationoverv iew.asp

49...Workers' Compensation Medicare Set-aside Arrangements (WCMSAs)

Medicare has a priority right of recovery over any other entity to the proceeds of any settlement.

To the extent that Medicare has made any "conditional payments", Medicare will recover those payments pursuant to 42 C.F.R. §411.47. Pursuant to 42 C.F.R. §411.21, "conditional payments" are Medicare payments for services for which another payer is responsible, made either on the bases set forth in 42 C.F.R. §411 subparts C through H, or because the intermediary or carrier did not know that the other coverage existed.[50]

◆Medicare Review

The regulations also state that CMS has the right to review the amount of the set-aside. But, as a practical matter, CMS limits its review to two qualifications, qualifications which CMS is constantly changing:

1. The claimant is currently a Medicare beneficiary and the total settlement amount is greater than $25,000;

2. The claimant has a 'reasonable expectation' of Medicare enrollment within 30 months of the settlement date and the anticipated total settlement amount for future medical expenses and disability/lost wages over the life or duration of the settlement agreement is expected to be greater than $250,000.

In fact, CMS may review the settlement, whether or not it meets the above qualifications, if it feels that the financial structure may result in Medicare paying for future expenses that should be covered by the §32 agreement.

Yet, as every workers compensation attorney will explain, the rules change from month to month and from one CMS regional office to the next. And, while CMS will issue a letter confirming that the §32 agreement is OK, it will only do so if the §32 agreement meets its standards for review. However, CMS will not provide the settling parties with '*verification*' letters confirming that approval of a particular Medicare set-aside arrangement is unnecessary. This creates a problem in that the lack of an answer can mean either (a) that CMS is still reviewing

---

50...www.cms.gov/WorkersCompAgencyServices/02_workerscompensationoverv iew.asp

the settlement in which case the completion of the agreement must wait or (b) that no approval is necessary so that there is no reason to delay the settlement.

◆How is the Set-Aside calculated?

Based on its experience with thousands, if not tens of thousands of claims, for injured workers with medical issues similar to that of the claimant, the carrier is able to fairly accurately calculate what will be its future costs for providing medical treatment to that claimant. And it is this sum that is used as part of the carrier's formula to determine what amount to offer the claimant as a settlement to close the case.

Medicare uses the same system. But rather than do the calculations on its own, very often the amounts calculated to be necessary for the set-aside are calculated by private sector companies which specialize in making these calculations. Lest the claimant think that the '*fix*' is in in these calculations, it is important to understand that if the calculation for the set-aside is too low, there will not be enough money in the set-aide for paying medical bills. And if the calculation for the set-aside is too high, it will be cheaper for the carrier to keep paying the bills rather than settle. So, it is in the interest of everyone that the calculation for the set-aside be as accurate and reliable as possible.

Nonetheless, I have seen some amounts for the set-aside that defy common sense:

> In November 2005, a §32 was set for a meeting because the Medicare set-aside was $53,999 out of a $64,350 settlement, which after a legal fee of $9,652.50 would leave the claimant with $698.50 if he put the set-aside into a special account as requested by CMS. But, for various reasons not discussed at the hearing, there was no requirement that the Medicare set-aside of $53,999 in this case be put into an escrow account.

> In the off-the-record discussion, the carrier's representative showed me a schedule of projected medical expenses attributed to this case by a third party actuary employed by the carrier to estimate Medicare set-asides. This claimant had a number of injuries from his three Workers Compensation cases being settled in this agreement and the schedule showed the anticipated future costs

which were calculated to be $53,999. What was most interesting was that the schedule included expenses for medical treatment for sites not established in the claim but anticipated to be consequential in the future.

In this case, the claimant had injuries to both of his hands so the schedule anticipated future Carpal Tunnel Syndrome to his wrists as well as eventual problems with his arms and then his shoulders. This actuarial schedule was considered a '*trade secret*' and was not a part of the agreement but rather just a method used to do some of the calculations necessary for the carrier to make its offer.

For that matter, the amount of the set-aside was mentioned for informational purposes in the §32 and was not legally relevant in my consideration of the §32. But it did raise an interesting point about the results of an actuarial schedule in excess of the total amount of the agreement. Then again, there may have been settlement discussions that failed because the set-aside was higher than the total amount of what the carrier was willing to offer: if CMS demands a set-aside higher than the settlement amount, before or after the legal fee, it is likely that the carrier does not enter into an agreement.

◆What happens to the Set-Aside funds?

CMS usually recommends but does not usually require that these funds be deposited into an interest-bearing account and that the claimant keep detailed records of all withdrawals for payment of bills that are related to the work-related injuries, including consequential injuries. (See page 106 in Chapter 14 - *Frequently Asked Questions* for a definition of '*consequential*'.) These records would prove to CMS that the funds allocated in the §32 for medical expenses were properly used.

However, it was rare that that portion of the settlement set aside for Medicare would have been deposited into a bank account or even that the agreement required the claimant do so after the claimant got the settlement check from the carrier. Once the agreement was approved and the check sent to the claimant, the legal issue of whether or not the claimant had to or should have put that set-aside into a special checking account was no longer under the Board's jurisdiction: the case was closed and this issue was no longer a Board problem.

Whether CMS, Medicare, new federal regulations, or the carrier will require a special account is an issue that may be affected by changes in the laws or in specific contractual agreements. But that is an issue to be discussed by the claimant with his attorney to determine whether a separate bank account is necessary or required.

◆Non-work related medical needs

If the claimant has a medical problem that is not related to the work-place injury, the claimant would receive coverage for this non-work related injury from Medicare, or for that matter, any other carrier as if there was no §32 settlement or work-related injury. This is why it is important to make sure that the correct sites of injury are listed in the §32 agreement and that sites of injury originally listed as part of the claim and later disallowed are specifically described in the agreement as *'disallowed.'*

◆When the Set-Aside is gone

Once the set-aside funds are depleted in a manner satisfactory to CMS, Medicare may then include the work-related injuries covered by the agreement under the claimant's regular Medicare program.

◆Summary

Like all laws, Title 42 Public Health Law is a very complex document and is subject to continuing modifications in its wording as well as interpretations of what that wording means. Also, the manner in which CMS deals with workers compensation cases varies depending on its backlog, often as bad as that of the NYS Workers Compensation Board.

But for those claimants whose age and medical condition could qualify them for a formal Medicare set-aside, there are no options. Federal regulations are quite strict and both the carrier and the claimant's attorney are held responsible under CMS regulations to insure compliance with CMS's rules and regulations.

But over and above CMS and its legally required and formal set-aside, the claimant must understand that this medical set-aside is not an accounting or financial gimmick. It is a formal acknowledgment by the carrier and claimant that, as a part of the settlement to close the case, the carrier is giving to the claimant a certain sum of money, the set-aside, which the carrier would have had to set aside to pay the claimant's future medical expenses if the claim had not been closed with a §32 settlement. It makes sense then that the claimant would follow the advice of CMS and put that money aside for future medical expenses. If that money is spent on other items, be it rent or a 48 inch LCD TV, when the claimant seeks to have Medicare pay for medical treatment for the injury covered under the §32 agreement, the claimant will encunter delays in getting that treatment as well as financial difficulties if Medicare or private health carriers will not pay the costs.

That set-aside is there for the benefit of the injured worker. Like the compensation portion of the settlement, the money for the §32 settlement should not be treated as a pot-of-gold at the end of the rainbow. To do so means that when the claimant seeks to use that money for appropriate medical treatment, goes to that pot, and finds that it is empty, what is in its place is a nice deep hole. And neither the Board nor the original carrier will help the claimant climb out of that hole.

CʒᏰᎤCʒᏰᎤCʒᏰᎤCʒᏰᎤ

Chapter 14
FREQUENTLY ASKED QUESTIONS.

If you started in the front of this book, you will have found answers to most of the following questions. But if you are like many, including me, and do not start at the beginning, these are some of the more frequent questions I get. Where appropriate, the answers that follow refer you to the chapter in this book that goes into more detail on the subject.

1. What if I have more than one case?

You can settle as many of your cases as you want and leave some open if you want. As a rule of thumb, most carriers will seek to close all your open cases in one settlement. The most cases I have ever seen settled in one agreement was eighteen that were established and six that were being controverted.

2. What if more than one carrier is involved?

They can all get together to determine each one's share. Sometimes, the one with the major case will make all the payments and the other carriers will just sign off. But, whatever arrangements are made between the carriers, your concern should only be what you get, not how the carriers split it up.

3. If I am a widow(er) can I settle my portion and not my children's portion of the claim?

Yes. Under §16(2), the weekly benefits of the deceased are divided between the surviving spouse (55%) and the children (45% split between the children if there are more than one). Therefore, the widow(er) can settle their portion of the claim under a §32 and not that of the minors. Details on this complex issue can be found in Chapter 5 - *Issues Resolved by §32's*, on page 43, 'Minor Children'.

4. Can you have two cases covering the same site of injury and settle only one?

Yes.

You can settle only one case. But the carrier whose case is still open will, in the future, argue that any lost wages, increases in compensation, or medical treatment are due to the injury from the case that was closed under the §32 settlement, not the open case for which it is responsible. Ultimately a law judge will make a decision with one of the following three results: (1) the carrier for the open case is 100% responsible, (2) everything is related to the case you settled by the §32 agreement and you are 100% responsible, or (3) it is apportioned by the law judge between the two cases, with the carrier of the open case being responsible for its share and you for the balance, out of the proceeds of your §32 settlement.

5. What is the difference between a '*Consequential*' injury and a '*Causally Related*' injury?

Let us assume that you tripped when your foot got stuck in a hole and you badly broke your ankle. A few days later when the swelling and pain from the ankle goes down, you and your doctor realize two bones in the foot were broken as well. About a month later when you are hobbling around on your crutches, you slip and fall and break your left wrist.

The two bones in your foot are '*causally related*' because these injuries occurred at the same time as the broken ankle. This holds true even if no one is aware of these original sites of injury for weeks after the original incident.

Your left wrist is a '*consequential*' injury because it is a consequence of having had the earlier injury.

Sometimes, a consequential injury can occur a few weeks after the initial injury but a causally related injury may not be apparent for months. While the laws relating to how these become a part of your claim differ, once the sites are included in your claim, bills relating to medical treatment for both are treated the same.

6. What happens if there is an appeal in process on an issue we are resolving with the §32 agreement?

All of the hearings, including the process of resolving an issue currently being appealed, are brought to a halt, as noted in NYCRR 300.36(c) which says that "*The receipt of an agreement by the board shall act as a stay on all proceedings before the board.*" If the settlement is approved, no decision is issued as a §32 agreement has resolved the issue. If the §32 is withdrawn or rejected, the hearing process and appeal process continue as if the negotiations never took place.

7. <u>Can I change my mind once the settlement is approved?</u>

Yes, you have 10 days from the date of the hearing. After that, it is too late. At the hearing, ask the law judge/commissioner for the actual day of the month which is the deadline. I made it a practice to give a specific date as it emphasized the point that there was a deadline and it was real.

8. <u>Can I ever get my case reopened?</u>

No. Not only will the Board not allow the case to be reopened, but all civil courts take the position that §32 agreements are under the Workers Compensation Law, thus not within their jurisdiction, and will refer you back to the Board. Any civil court judge who decided that he does have the jurisdiction will more than likely find this decision making its way to the Appellate Court where it would undoubtedly be reversed. Appendix J - *Closed means 'CLOSED'* starting on page 141 emphasizes how the law is interpreted to mean the case can not be reopened.

9. <u>What if there are questions about the interpretation of the agreement?</u>

I am aware of only a few cases in which there were disputes as to the meaning of the §32 agreement. And all these were the result of information about sites of injury not being made clear, thus leaving open the question(s) as to who is responsible for paying bills for treatment to those sites of injury.

The Board will not resolve such disputes, taking the position that the case(s) has been closed and no longer within the jurisdiction of the Board. I have argued that if the Board paid more attention to the contents of some of the §32's in which such information about sites of injury and medical bills are not clear and took the time at the settlement hearing to resolve the potential confusions, there would be no disputes after the case is closed.

These cases end up in civil court on the grounds that there is a *'contractual dispute'* to be resolved. And, the claimant must hire and pay for an attorney out of his own pocket.

As noted in Chapter 3 - *A Basic §32 Agreement* (page 20) and Chapter 7 - *Medical Expenses* (page 63), attention in negotiating and drafting the agreement should insure the proper list of sites of injury and payment of medical expenses, past and future. Had this been done in the disputed cases, there would have been no dispute or misunderstandings.

10. What if after the settlement, I find some Out-of-pocket expenses I forgot to hand in for reimbursement?

Unless the carrier is in a *'giving'* mood, you will not get reimbursed. So make sure to collect all these expenses and submit them during the negotiations. Showing up with them at the hearing itself could result in the carrier walking out or offering you only a small settlement for those expenses.

11. What if my medical provider has not sent in all his bills by the date of the settlement?

That is not your concern if it is for treatment for your work-related injury. The late submission of bills is between the doctor and the carrier. By law, the doctor has a time limit within which to submit those bills; if not, the carrier can refuse to pay them and the medical provider, who cannot collect from you, loses that money.

12. What if I need expensive surgery which no one contemplated at the time of the settlement?

The carrier will not be responsible. Either you must pay or hope that Medicare or your private health insurance will pay. See Chapter 7 - *Medical Expenses*, page 63 for more details.

13. What if my private health carrier or Medicare insists that the treatment I need is covered by my §32 settlement and won't pay for it?

That is a dispute between you and the private health insurance and/or Medicare. And, while a properly written §32 should make it easy for that determination to be made, everyone knows that carriers and Medicare will use any excuse they can to deny a legitimate claim. But to seek a resolution, you must go through the standard appeals process offered by your private health insurance company or Medicare. You will not be able to go back to the workers compensation system to help you resolve the dispute.

14. <u>What if they insist I pay for my treatment & I don't have the money?</u>

There is no standard answer to this question and it is not one that can be answered by the workers compensation system because by taking the §32 settlement any issues you may have had that relate to your work-related injury can not be resolved under the jurisdiction of the Workers Compensation Board - that is the law. So, your only alterative is to do whatever it is that you would have done if you needed medical care for a non-work related injury and did not have insurance and the financial means with which to pay for it. The answer to that question is beyond the scope of this book.

15. <u>If I accept an agreement, what is the latest I can change my mind?</u>

Under the current law it is 10 days from the date the §32 is approved. But ask your attorney or the law judge for a fixed date. But if you do change your mind at the last minute, do not expect your attorney to be overjoyed (unless he counseled against your taking the §32, which some have done). And the carrier will certainly not make another offer to you again. It does cost the carrier time for a member of their staff or an attorney to prepare all the papers and carriers do not like having all that work rejected at the last minute.

16. <u>Can anyone stop me from getting the settlement or interfere in the negotiations?</u>

Legally, no. See Chapter 12 - *Who Participates in the Agreement*, page 92. But I always suggest keeping the spouse up to date, unless perhaps you communicate through a divorce attorney. No one can stop the settlement, other than the law judge. But, as noted in Chapter 11 - *Is the money all yours?* on page 84, money can be withheld from your settlement if you are past due on child support payments or have other specifically noted liens on your claim.

17. <u>Can anyone take the settlement money away from me?</u>

Other than a few limited liens, the Board can not legally allow any deductions or claims against your settlement. But, once you deposit the check, that is another matter. See Chapter 11 - *Is the Money All Yours?*, page 84

18. <u>Do I pay income taxes on the money I get from a settlement?</u>

Usually not. But with the tax laws at both the federal, state, and local level changing constantly, you would have to check with your attorney and/or accountant. See more information in Chapter 11 - *Is the money all yours?*, page 84.

19. <u>Can anyone find out the size of my settlement or see the actual agreement?</u>

No, not unless they have a legal right to do so.

But what does '*legal right*' mean?

If you seek to have medical treatment covered by a private health insurance plan and it thinks that your injuries were work- related and covered by workers compensation insurance, it may ask to see the agreement. The federal, state, or locality (if the latter has an income tax) may ask questions about your finances, particularly if you have a large settlement. If you are involved in divorce proceeding or a law suit, you may be asked questions about your settlement. Ask your attorney how much of the agreement you must show them.

If you ask Medicare to pay for medical treatment, it has the right to ask to see your agreement. See Chapter 13 - *Medicare & Set Asides*, page 98.

Your employer, as an '*interested party*' and not a '*party of interest*' has no legal right to demand you give him a copy of the contract. But he can get it from the insurance company who is his agent under the insurance policy.

20. <u>Can I return to work?</u>

Yes. In fact, if you could have returned to work earlier, you should have done so. You make more money working than you get from workers compensation even if you get the maximum award allowed by law. The maximum weekly award you could get before 2007 was $400 for which you had to be making $600 or more weekly. Since 2007, that rate has increased from $400 and is indexed with a wage rated supplied by the New York State Department of Labor based on New York States average weekly wage.

Why was 1/3 deducted?

When these formulas were done, it was estimated that you paid about 1/3 of your salary in taxes: state, city, federal income tax and social security. In actuality, most taxpayers pay less than a 1/3 in taxes. Consequently, if you went back to work and earned the $600 as salary, you would have more in your pocket after taxes than that tax free $400 maximum compensation award. And you would not have to concern yourself with a carrier trying to cut your benefits. Also, you would not have to worry about being replaced by your employer while you recover from your injury. Remember: workers compensation awards are '*temporary replacement*' income, not an alternative life stye.

And for the majority of people, working is emotionally and psychologically better for you than sitting home bemoaning your injury.

And for those who think that they can get a job '*under the table*' and still collect workers compensation, carriers are very aggressive in seeking out those who commit this kind of fraud, for which penalties are severe, both criminal and civil, along with a permanent black mark on your record!!

21. <u>Does the settlement affect my Social Security or Medicare?</u>

Yes. As for your Medicare, there is an entire chapter devoted to the issue which probably raises more questions than it does answers. This is an area of federal law that changes every few weeks and the impact that '*Obamacare*' will have is yet to be fully understood.

Even if you currently get Social Security or Social Security Disability and whether or not your compensation rate from either is already adjusted based on your prior workers compensation awards, the settlement could have an impact.

These two issues are just two of the many that support my recommendation that you get an attorney to assist in the negotiations.

22. What is *'Money Moving'*?

That is a term which refers to the actual check that is sent out by the carrier to you to bring your account up to date.

Let us assume that you have been getting a temporary rate of $200 a week for 30 weeks ($6,000) but no legal fees have been awarded yet. The law judge then sets a permanent rate of $300 per week and awards a $500 legal fee, $250 of out *'money moving'* and the balance of $250 out of future weekly payments. You will get a check for $2,750, the amount of *'money moving'*: 30 prior weeks at an additional $100 per week = $3,000 less the $250 legal fee = $2,750. Thus *'money moving'* is the amount of the check being sent to you after various adjustments.

CRURCRURCRURCRU

Chapter 15
A FEW FINAL WORDS

Now that you have concluded this book, the question is:

Have you come to a conclusion regarding your potential §32 offer?

Perhaps for every answer given in this book, there are more questions not answered.

But you, as the reader, must understand that this book is not addressed to YOU as an individual but to YOU as a group, the community of injured workers as well as your family members, attorneys who specialize in other areas of law, and members of the workers compensation community.

As I mentioned earlier in this book, while there tend to be similarities between cases, a closer examination will show that no two cases are alike. Even if we have two claimants working for the same company who are the same age, earning the same salary, and having identical injuries, the fact that one is located in New York City and the other is located in an economically faltering community upstate will mean that there are differences in the probability of a return to the workplace. And this could mean a difference in the level of compensation as the case continues.

These differences, which may not be apparent to the person who is inexperienced in workers compensation law, can make a major difference not only in the terms of the settlement but even whether a settlement is appropriate. Throughout this book and in the appendixes that follow, there are references to court decisions, workers compensation law, and the rules and regulations by which the New York State Workers Compensation Board processes and adjudicates claims and interprets the law.

There was a major philosophical shift in 1996 when the New York State workers compensation law was changed to allow a case to be closed, a philosophy not accepted by all of the commissioners. Changes in medicine, rehabilitation techniques, and economic conditions will continue to compel a reassessment of the current laws and statutes pertaining to workers compensation. And more often than not, the philosophy of the political parties in power at that time will strengthen or change the direction of how the Board adjudicates controversies and interprets the law.

Because of the complexity of the laws, the unique aspect of each claim, and the constantly evolving interpretation of the law, you, as the injured worker, are best served by having in experienced, knowledgeable advocate at your side: an attorney specializing in workers compensation or a licensed representative, a non-attorney authorized by the New York State Workers Compensation Board to act as an attorney in virtually all matters relating to workers compensation issues.

The choices you will make are not easy and they should not be.

Many of you have been dependent upon your awards of compensation to supplement lost income and to pay for the medical bills necessary to treat your work-related injury. For many injured workers, there is a comfort in these guarantees although changing circumstances in the course of your recovery could cause either to end. On the other hand, closing the case is a good way to close a chapter in one's life and, with this settlement, get a fresh start in life.

It is my hope that this book will help you make a decision such that, three years after you agreed to accept a settlement or decide not to take one, you will feel that when you made that decision you had all the information necessary to make what at that time was the best possible choice you could have made.

Good luck.

Michael T. Berns

APPENDIXES

CRUCRUCRUCRU

116

APPENDIX A
The 10 Basic Questions for the §32 Hearing

SECTION 32 SETTLEMENT AGREEMENT
CLAIMANT RELEASE
Form C-32.1 (1-11)
After reviewing and signing the final Section 32 Settlement Agreement, claimant must complete this document and have it notarized. In order to expedite the processing of the Agreement, this document must be submitted to the Board along with the Section 32 Agreement (Form C32). See the reverse side for more information about the Section 32 process.

1. Do you understand that the Section 32 agreement, if approved by the Board, is binding on you and all the other parties and may not be appealed to either the Board or the Courts?
2. Do you understand that once the agreement has been approved by the Board and the ten day waiting period has expired, the agreement cannot be withdrawn, modified, or reopened, and that the only way an approved agreement can be revisited is upon a written request to the Board, with the approval of all parties to the agreement, and the approval of the Board?
3. Have you been placed in any duress in order to accept this agreement?
4. Have you been made any promises that are not reflected in this agreement?
5. Are there any outstanding liens on your claim(s) (such as child support, taxes, spousal maintenance, or attorney fees)?
6. Do you understand that you have the right to litigate your workers compensation claim(s), and that you do not have to settle your claim(s)?
7. Do you understand and accept the amount of the settlement?
8. Do you agree to the fee requested by your attorney or licensed representative with the understanding that the Board has the authority to approve, disapprove, or modify the fee requested?
9. Do you understand that when this agreement becomes final, any future medical expenses related to this claim may become your responsibility?
10. Have any doctor/hospital bills related to this claim been paid by anyone other than your employer or the workers compensation insurance carrier?

CRECRECRECRE

APPENDIX B
My Lump Sum Speech

This my version of the speech given at one time at the start of the hearings to those claimants who were seeking to partially close their case with a Lump Sum Settlement, which, until 1996, was the only way to 'close' a case - see Chapter 2 - Settlements Prior to §32's, starting on page 12.

My name is Michael Berns and I am the Commissioner who has been designated to act on behalf of the Workers Compensation Board to conduct these hearings and to approve or disapprove the proposed settlement agreed to by you and the insurance company

Ladies and gentlemen, your cases have reached the point where they are being considered for settlement on a lump sum payment basis under Section 15, Subdivision 5b, of the Workers' Compensation Law.

I will explain to you as a group what will take place here today at the hearing so that you will understand what is happening. If you have any questions or comments, please hold them until your particular case is called and then I will be happy to hear what you wish to say.

Your agreement with the insurance company to settle your Compensation case is subject to Board approval. You should be advised that the Board does not approve every application it considers. We will approve it if we find that the settlement is fair and in the best interest to you, the claimant. In order for me to determine that, I will have to ask you a number of questions that seem personal in nature, but I need to know the answers in order to approve the settlement.

Because you have been found to have a permanent partial disability, the Board has determined that your injury has cut back on your earnings capacity and you are now being given weekly compensation to make up for what has been judged to be your lower weekly earnings ability. By taking this lump sum settlement, you give up two benefits: 1st is access to any and all future medical benefits and 2nd you are exchanging this guaranteed weekly payment for a one-time lump-sum payment. If for any reason you should spend or lose that lump sum payment being decided today, you will have spent or lost that money. And you will not be able to reopen your case just to get that money back.

To repeat, if your settlement is approved today, there will be no more weekly or biweekly compensation payments to you.

If your settlement is approved, there will be no further payment of medical bills or hospital charges or any other expense for medical treatment. And you cannot get surgery or other medical treatment under your spouse's policy or any other policy as your original injury was covered by workers' compensation. If you attempt to get coverage under another policy, if the insurance company finds out what you are doing, they can not only demand all their money back but they can also cancel the policy and you may be subject to legal penalties. You will have to pay for any and all future medical expenses which are related to the injuries from this claim.

The Board may consider an application to re-open your case, but only if all three of the following conditions are met:

1. You, the claimant, must prove that your condition has become worse than it is today

2. The change for the worse in your condition must be due to this accident and no other cause.

3. The change in your condition is in no way found in the current medical evidence, and, therefore, not considered or contemplated by the Board in closing your case today.

   • For example, if your doctor recommends surgery or further treatment and you refuse it, you cannot get coverage for this in the future because it has been considered in closing your case today and/or has been mentioned in the current medical reports in your file. And you could end up using most, if not all, of your Lump Sum settlement to pay those medical expenses.

   • If you have a bad back or knee and have another accident which is not work related, any medical expenses caused by the new accident for your old injury will have to be paid for by you or the insurance company involved in the new accident.

   • If you have a back or knee or leg problem and are limping and in 3, 5, or even 20 years have to use crutches to walk, that is something which could be anticipated from your injury and you're getting older and most likely a re-opening would be denied. But if you need a wheel chair to get around, then there is the possibility, not a certainty, that your case would be reopened.

These three conditions are difficult for you to prove and you must pay for all medical expenses to prove that your case should be re-opened. Another purpose of today's hearing is to indicate on the records, by your testimony, that you agree with the doctor that you do not need and are not getting any further medical treatment and that your condition has reached maximum medical improvement.

If the case is reopened, the insurance company must begin paying expenses for medical treatment after reopening the case without any reference to the lump sum payment being approved today.

But in order to get compensation again, there are time limits for reopening your case: 18 years from the date of accident and eight years from the date of last payment of compensation in your case. Your attorney can give you the details. The 18 years begins to run from the date of your accident. To calculate the eight years, the lump sum payment is extended into the future at a weekly rate, called the 'allocation rate' and that is when the eight years begin to run. I will give you your allocation rate when we hear you case later today.

If you apply to reopen your case within the time limits and the Board approves the reopening, then when today's settlement is set aside, the insurance company is given credit for the amount of the lump sum payment paid to you.

If you apply to reopen your case after the time limits by meeting the three requirements I mentioned earlier, then the Board will deny your application for further compensation payments although you can still get payment of medical bills.

Insofar as today's agreement is concerned, those of you who are represented by an attorney or licensed representative know that they are asking for a fee for the work done negotiating this settlement. This fee, which will be deducted from your settlement and sent to your representative by separate check by the insurance company, is usually

10% of the settlement plus $100. However, please understand that the fee is coming out of the money you are getting today and is subject to your approval that your attorney's representation of you during your case deserves the fee he is requesting. I have the legal authority to approve the fee that he requested or to reduce it, if that is appropriate. Also remember that it is unlawful in New York State for an attorney or representative to receive any other fee in this case other than the one that I approve later today or that has previously been approved by a Workers comp Law Judge.

If you have any doubts or concerns about closing your case today, you may withdraw your application today or postpone it to a later date, by asking for an adjournment. And this decision will have no influence on the Board, if and when you decide to purse this matter at a later date.

CRROCRROCRROCRRO

APPENDIX C
My Lump Sum Hearing Questions

1. Calling case #_____
2. For the record, will everyone appearing, please give their names.
3. Raise your right hand ... do you promise that the testimony you are about to give here today is the truth?
   Please speak up so that the court reporter can hear your answers.
4. For the records, please state your name and your mailing address, and the names of other parties with you in the room today.
5. Will you look at the C-22 form[51] on which today's hearing is based and confirm for the record that it is your signature on the back of the form.
6. This case is established for injuries to your _____, injuries from an accident dated _____.
7. Do you have any other open claims or cases before Workers' Compensation at this time?
8. Has this §15-5b settlement previously been before a Commissioner?
9. When was the last time that you were treated by a doctor for the injury in question?
10. Were you discharged from any further medical treatment at that time?
11. Do you take any medications as a result of your injury?
12. Is there a letter from the claimant's doctor showing the patient has been discharged.
13. *Is there something in the records which show that this claimant has a PERMANENT PARTIAL DISABILITY (PPD)[52]*
    a. Let the record show a letter dated from Dr showing _____
    b. Are there any objections to this letter being accepted as evidence?
    c. Fine, then the letter of discharge is made part of the record. Based on the total record, the claimant is found to have a permanent partial disability.
14. Is anyone aware of any unpaid medical bills?
15. Mr/Mrs/Ms_____ , please state for the record the amount upon which you have agreed to settle?

51...Unlike the §32 agreement, the Lump Sum Agreement was a fill-in-the-blanks form designed by the Board and required to be used for EVERY Lump SUM Settlement.

52...A PPD was a requirement to qualify for a lump sum settlement.

16. Are you currently working, if so as of what date_____?[53]
    a. What type of work is it, & this job's weekly salary?
    b. Do you have any other of income?
    c. Does your spouse work, if so at what & what $?
17. Do you support anyone on your income?
18. What do you plan to do with the $$ you will receive?
19. Can you & your family manage without the $ you now receive
    weekly from the insurance company?
20. Are there any third party actions being considered? Are you suing
anyone as a result of this accident?
21. Do you have any unpaid child support or tax liens against you at this
time?
22. These answers satisfy all my concerns regarding financial issues?
23. Now to the issue of awards. According to the C-22 form, the last
awards ran from ____ to_____. Is that correct? Based on this settlement,
awards will run from __Date__ through And the allocation rate is set at
$____.
24. Have all legal bills been paid?
25. Your attorney is asking for a fee for the work done settling this case,
of $_____, which will be deducted from the amount you have agreed to
accept from the insurance company. Is this fee acceptable to you?
26. You were present earlier when I explained to you, in my speech, what
it means to close a case on a lump sum settlement. Did you understand
me?
28. Do you have any questions you need to ask me about your worker's
compensation case?
29. Are there any unresolved issues in this case?
30. All right. This is the decision in the case of WCB#_____.

> A lump sum in the amount of $_____ is approved, with a lien
> thereon in the amount of $____, payable as a fee to the claimant's
> attorney. The additional awards are brought up to date from _____
> through _____ at the rate of $_____ weekly Reduced Earnings
> and that is the allocation rate.

CRROCRROCRROCRRO

53...Unlike §32 agreement, the personal financial status of the claimant and their
family was to be taken into account when considering the approval of a lump sum
agreement.

APPENDIX D

WAMO Guidelines

[The guidelines as issued by the New York State Workers Compensation Board, dated August 24, 2010]

Among the goals of the 2007 Workers' Compensation Reform Legislation are increasing benefits to injured workers, implementing cost-savings, and closing the Special Disability Fund to new cases. The addition of subdivisions (e), (f), (g), (h), and (i) to Workers' Compensation Law ('WCL') Section 32 will assist in attaining those goals. The Waiver Agreement Management Office ('WAMO'), on behalf of the Special Disability Fund[54], may enter into waiver agreements to resolve workers compensation claims, utilizing funds generated by the proceeds of bonds sold by the Dormitory Authority of the State of New York. Creation of WAMO will encourage fair settlements of claims involving the Special Disability Fund. Such settlements will aid the statutory design to reduce the liabilities and ultimately close-out the Special Disability Fund. Such settlements will initially stabilize and ultimately reduce assessments and thereby lower the cost of providing compensation insurance. Those actions will in turn result in an improved business climate and increased employment opportunities in New York State.

GUIDELINES

The following Guidelines will be followed by WAMO in negotiating and seeking Board approval of waiver agreements (WCL §32(e)). These Guidelines shall also be followed by any third party with whom WAMO may contract to manage, administer, or settle claims on its behalf (WCL §32 (i) (1)).

1) In accordance with WCL §32 (b) (1), (2), no waiver agreement proposed by WAMO, or any third party with whom WAMO may contract to manage, administer, or settle claims on its behalf, shall be unfair, unconscionable or improper as a matter of law; nor shall any waiver agreement proposed by WAMO be based upon

---

54...One of the many insurance funds established by the State of New York to reimburse the regular carrier under a specific set of conditions. See page 92 in Chapter 12- _Who participates in the Agreement?_

intentional misrepresentation of material fact.

2) To the extent that there is established Special Disability Fund liability involved, WAMO will cooperate with all insurance carriers as defined in WCL §2(12) in meeting their obligation under WCL §32(a) to offer each claimant the opportunity to enter into a waiver agreement within two years after the date the claim was indexed by the Board or six months after the claimant is classified with a permanent disability, whichever is later, and in the case of death, within six months after entitlement to benefits is established for all beneficiaries. WAMO shall further cooperate with any insurance carrier, self-insured employer or the State Insurance Fund in apportioning responsibility for making payments under such agreements. Any such agreement shall clearly set forth the individual payment obligations of the signatories, or shall signify that all signatories are jointly and severally liable.

3) In compliance with WCL §32(a), any waiver agreement offer made by WAMO shall clearly state what portion of the offer is for:

    a) Compensation, as defined in WCL §2(6), if any.
    b) Medical benefits, including prescription medicine, if any.
    c) Fee of claimant's attorney or licensed representative, if any.

4) If the claimant is not represented by an attorney or licensed representative, any waiver agreement offered by WAMO to the claimant shall be accompanied by a written statement of claimant's rights, obligations and potential liability if the offer is accepted.

5) In negotiating waiver agreements, WAMO will balance competing interests: providing fair settlements for claimants while acting within the financial interest of the Special Disability Fund. WAMO will also assist in meeting the statutory goal of closing out the Special Disability Fund. Therefore, WAMO will make waiver agreement offers to claimants in appropriate cases and receive, review, analyze, and respond to waiver agreement offers made to WAMO by and on behalf of claimants.

6) WAMO's jurisdiction extends to cases with established Special Disability Fund liability under both WCL §15(8) ('second injury fund') and WCL §14(6) ('concurrent employment fund'). It is

therefore evident that WAMO's cases will be quite diverse: some will involve permanently disabled claimants, some will not; some will involve anticipated continuing benefits for both indemnity and medical expenses, some will involve only continuing indemnity or only continuing medical benefits; and therefore, some cases will require Medicare Set-Aside Agreements and some will not. Within each of the foregoing sets of cases, individual cases will have distinct facts and circumstances to be considered in the negotiation of appropriate waiver agreements. In view of such diversity of cases, it is not feasible to create a settlement formula that would fit every case. Instead, WAMO will analyze each case on its merits, giving due consideration to the following list of issues:

a) Anticipated duration and amount of future Special Disability Fund exposure.

b) Whether claimant has been classified as permanently disabled.

c) Current weekly indemnity rate.

d) Claimant's present medical condition and prognosis; recent treatment history; current prescription medication regimen; and reasonably projected future medical costs.

e) Claimant's life expectancy and whether it is impacted by unrelated medical condition(s).

f) Other sources of income.
   i. Pension
   ii. Income of Spouse
   iii. Other

g) Whether there are unresolved issues in the case relative to WCL §114-a[55].

h) Whether claimant is a current Medicare recipient, or is anticipated to become a Medicare recipient within thirty (30) months.
   i. If either scenario applies, see Guideline #8 below.

i) Whether the case involves a pending or reasonably anticipated third party action. (See: WCL §29).

j) It is not intended that the foregoing list of issues and circumstances be considered exclusive or exhaustive. WAMO will consider any and all relevant facts and circumstances in determining whether a waiver agreement is appropriate in each case and, if so, the appropriate amount to be paid pursuant to such agreement.

55...§114-a refers to fraud issues

7) If the claim to be resolved via a waiver agreement is a death claim, WAMO must ascertain the identity of all eligible beneficiaries and confirm that all are parties to the proposed waiver agreement. Where infant beneficiaries are involved, confirm that all appropriate steps are taken to protect their interests and ensure that the waiver agreement is binding upon them.

8) Before entering into a proposed waiver agreement, which exceeds seven (7) years of indemnity benefits (plus funds for a reasonable medical allocation or Medicare Set-aside, where applicable), WAMO will obtain confirmation from an appropriate financial professional that the proposed waiver agreement is within the best financial interest of the Special Disability Fund.

9) Medicare's interests must be considered in the context of the settlement of workers compensation claims via waiver agreements pursuant to WCL §32. Therefore, WAMO shall be cognizant of all statutes, rules and regulations pertaining to the interplay of Medicare and WCL §32 settlements; and WAMO shall not enter into waiver agreements under WCL §32 wherein Medicare has viable interests and those interests are not considered and addressed. In particular, if claimant is a current Medicare recipient, or is anticipated to become a Medicare recipient within thirty (30) months, and if the proposed WCL §32 waiver agreement will extinguish claimant's right to further causally related medical benefits in the compensation claim, WAMO shall obtain prior approval from Medicare before seeking Board approval of a WCL §32 waiver agreement which includes termination of claimant's rights to future causally related medical benefits.

All claimants shall be duly advised of their responsibility to protect Medicare's interest when settling a claim by means of a WCL §32 waiver agreement. In particular, claimants who choose to protect Medicare's interest by means of a self administered Medicare set-aside account, will be duly advised of the requirement that such account be maintained separately from claimant's personal checking and savings accounts; and that such account be used solely for payment of causally related medical expenses that would otherwise be payable by Medicare. In addition, such claimants will be duly advised regarding the annual reporting requirements relative to self administered Medicare set-aside accounts.

10) In order to properly evaluate claims for the purpose of negotiating or managing waiver agreements, WAMO will require relevant data from insurance carriers, employers, the State Insurance Fund and the Special Funds Conservation Committee. In accordance with WCL §32(i)(4), WAMO shall issue written requests to the above referenced parties for any such relevant data that is lacking and necessary to an evaluation of the value of a claim. (See: Subject No. 046-310, issued April 21, 2009, for procedures to follow if the recipient of such request objects to disclosure.)

11) As set forth in WCL §32(e), WAMO may enter into waiver agreements without consulting with, or obtaining the approval of, any employer, insurance carrier, self-insurer, the State Insurance Fund, or the Special Funds Conservation Committee. However, as set forth in WCL §32(f), WAMO shall give written notice to any employer, insurance carrier or the State Insurance Fund entitled to receive reimbursement from the Special Disability Fund in regard to any claimant, of any waiver agreement signed by WAMO with such claimant within fourteen (14) days of submitting such waiver agreement to the Board for approval.

12) If a claimant seeks a WCL §32 waiver agreement with WAMO whereby only the indemnity portion of the claim is to be closed, WAMO will contact the carrier/self-insured employer to obtain an agreement to waive any potential future right to transfer liability for medical liability to the Special Fund for Reopened Cases under WCL §25-a. If the carrier/self-insured employer agrees to waive said WCL §25-a rights, that provision shall be incorporated into the WCL §32 waiver agreement and the carrier/self-insured employer shall be a party and signatory to the WCL §32 waiver agreement. Absent such agreement by the carrier/self-insured employer, WAMO will not enter into the proposed WCL §32 waiver agreement with the claimant.

13) WAMO will be added as a party of interest on each case in which WAMO will be paying all or any portion of a WCL §32 waiver agreement. Examiners in the Section 32 Workgroup of the Workers' Compensation Board shall review proposed waiver agreements to which WAMO is a party with the same level of scrutiny applied in their review of proposed settlement agreements submitted by all carriers, self-insured employers, and the State Insurance Fund.

Similarly, Workers' Compensation Law Judges shall review proposed waiver agreements to which WAMO is a party with the same level of scrutiny applied in their review of proposed settlement agreements submitted by all carriers, self-insured employers and the State Insurance Fund in determining whether to approve or disapprove the proposed settlement agreement.

14) WAMO representatives may appear by telephone conference or by video conference at the hearings scheduled for consideration of proposed waiver agreements.

15) Upon approval of waiver agreements to which WAMO is a party, timely payment shall be made of WAMO's liability pursuant to such agreements. (See Guideline #5 above regarding cases in which liability is apportioned between WAMO and one or more other parties.

CR∞CR∞CR∞CR∞

APPENDIX E
A Generic §32 Agreement

The parties, listed below, have decided to settle this claim under §32 of the Workers' Compensation Law. The claimant agrees that by participating in a §32 agreement, the claimant is waiving the right to have the Workers' Compensation Board determine, through litigation and/or the administrative hearing process, the right to continuing payments, value of the claim, and access to future medical treatment, which could result in the value of the claim and value of future medical treatment being greater than, less than, or equal to the value of this §32 agreement. The parties to this agreement are:

        Claimant _____
        Carrier _____
        on behalf of the employer_____
        Self-insured Employer _____
        Special Funds Conservation Committee _____

This settlement agreement is the culmination of the following history. This case is established for injuries to the claimant's _____ as the result of an accident of _____. The average weekly wage has been established at $_____. Based on the medical evidence in the file, at a hearing of _____, the Workers' Compensation Board classified the claimant as permanently partially disabled, symptomatic treatment was authorized, and carrier/Self-insured was directed to continue payments to the claimant at $_____ reduced earnings.

Repeat the above if more than one claim is being settled.

The carrier/Self-insured agrees to continue payments to the claimant at $_____ reduced earnings up until
      • the date of the hearing at which this agreement is approved or the date it is approved via an administrative decision.
      • the date final approval is issued by the Board.
      • the date of the filing of this agreement.
      • *Other date* _____

The carrier/Self-insured agrees to pay to the claimant the sum of $_____, in full and final settlement of all claims of workers' compensation indemnity and medical benefits. Said amount shall be payable within ten days after the filing of the Decision approving this Agreement. The award is allocated at the $_____ rate.

WAIVER FURTHER CLAIMS FOR COMPENSATION

The claimant hereby stipulates that there is no further claim for causally related disability, lost wages or reduced earning capacity that may arise subsequent to the date of approval of this settlement and that no additional claim shall be filed against the employer and/or its workers compensation carrier/Self-insured, directly or consequentially related to the injuries covered by this claim.

ONGOING MEDICAL

The carrier/Self-insured agrees to audit and pay for all medical bills, subject to medical arbitration and the New York Workers' Compensation Fee Schedule, for treatment of established, causally related sites of injury rendered prior to the approval date of this agreement. Payment of all other medical bills shall not be the responsibility of the carrier/self-insured. The carrier/Self-insured also agrees to withdraw all C-8.1 objections upon approval of this settlement agreement. The claimant also stipulates that there is no further claim for additional medical treatment, transportation, or miscellaneous expenses arising from this accident. The claimant further agrees that any need for medical treatment which may arise subsequent to the approval of this agreement will be the claimant's responsibility solely and not the responsibility of the employer and/or its workers compensation carrier/Self-insured.

SOCIAL SECURITY OFFSET
select one

•Upon entering into this §32 agreement, it is agreed by the parties that $_____ of the total consideration of this settlement is allocated for the claimant's future medical expenses related to the injuries referred to in this settlement pursuant to the Medicare as a Secondary Payer, statute 42 CFR 411.26 and 42 CFR 411.47.

•The claimant hereby acknowledges that they are not currently receiving nor applied for Social Security benefits in connection with the injuries arising from this claim established for the date of _____
　　Use this language rather than 'accident dated' in the

event it is an ODNCR.

FEE

The parties agree that an attorney's fee in the amount of $_____ will be deducted from the claimant's settlement as a lien and paid directly to the claimant's attorney ____Attorney name____ subject to the Workers' Compensation Board approval.

SPECIAL FUNDS CONSERVATION COMMITTEE
Select one

•Special Funds Conservation Committee agrees to reimburse the carrier/Self-insured $_____ of the settlement, subject to a finding of liability under Workers' Compensation Law §15(8)(d) and less any statutory retention period remaining at the time the agreement is approved. This consent is not to be construed a concession under Workers' Compensation Law §15(8)(d).

 •Special Funds Conservation Committee agrees to reimburse the carrier/Self-insured $_____ of the settlement, pursuant to §15-8___ §14-6____.

•The carrier/Self-insured agrees to withdraw its C-250 application pending approval of this settlement.

THIRD PARTY SUITS §29

•Although the parties are unaware of any pending third party action, the carrier/self-insured hereby reserves all rights to offsets and liens pursuant to §29, in relation to any third party action brought as a result of this claim.

•All parties acknowledge that a third party action brought as a result of this claim:

> *Select one*
> •has commenced and been taken into consideration by all parties in the above noted settlement and the Carrier/Self-insured agrees that it is **retaining all rights** to offsets and liens pursuant to §29.
>
> •has commenced and been taken into consideration by all parties in

the above noted settlement and the Carrier/Self-insured agrees that it is **waiving all rights** to offsets and liens pursuant to §29.

•**has been settled** with the result that the Carrier/Self-insured is taking a credit of $_____ to resolve any rights to offsets and liens pursuant to §29.

•**has been settled** and the settlement amount included in this agreement.

INCOME TAX - LIENS - ENGLISH LANGUAGE

All sums set forth above constitute damages on account of personal injuries arising from an occurrence within the meaning of Section 104(a)(1) of the Interval Revenue Code.

The claimant confirms that there are no liens for child support or alimony.

The claimant's attorney confirms that the claimant understands English and that there is no need for a translator to assist the claimant in understanding the terms and conditions of this agreement.

Before inserting this last paragraph, make sure claimant will not be using an interpreter as many non-native Americans will ask for an interpreter at a §32 hearing even if they have not used one previously and note that family members can not act as translators.

GENERAL RELEASE

In consideration for this settlement, the claimant and the claimant's heirs, executors, administrators, trustees, legal representatives and assigns hereby forever releases and discharges the employer and carrier/Self-insured and any of their past or present entities, subsidiaries, divisions, affiliates, related business entities, successors and assigns and their respective heirs, executors, administrators, trustees, legal representatives and assigns, from all claims, demands, causes of action and liabilities that were or could have been raised in conjunction with WCB case number _____.

The above constitutes the complete agreement of the parties for the resolution of all outstanding issues in the above workers compensation claim(s) and the parties attest that there are no other documents or agreements on which the signing of this agreement is contingent.

All parties agree that upon the approval of this settlement, the settlement will become final, irrevocable , and not subject to re-opening, reconsideration, or appeal except by written consent of both parties and approval of the Workers' Compensation Board. The claimant further agrees that the claimant will not apply to the Workers' Compensation Board for re-re-opening, reconsideration or appeal, notwithstanding any change in medical condition or earnings based upon the same common nucleus of operative facts which formed the basis of this claim. This settlement is final conclusive and binding on all parties.

_____   _____
Claimant (Signature)   Attorney or Lic. Rep (Signature)

_____   By_____
Carrier/Self-Insured/Employer   Attorney or Lic. Rep. (Signature)
      (Print name)

_____   By_____
Other Party - if any   Attorney or Lic. Rep. (Signature)
      (Print name)

_____   _____   _____
Commissioner/Law Judge   Title   Date
      (Signature)

[EDITOR'S NOTE: You are free to copy or scan this. But with all the changes taking place in the workers compensation law and the fact that I, who headed the group that drafted this provisional agreement, am not an attorney, you should seek formal legal advice before filling in the blanks and submitting it as a formal agreement.]

ᐧᔑᐧᔑᐧᔑᐧᔑ

APPENDIX F

Form C-4: The basic doctor's report, which as noted in the circled items below, shows fee for the services provided, the fee that the carrier pays. Once the settlement is complete, the doctor has no obligation to charge you the same.

DOCTOR'S REPORT AND EMPLOYER BILLING FORM

STATE OF NEW YORK
WORKERS' COMPENSATION BOARD

SERVICES PROVIDED UNDER WCB PREFERRED PROVIDER ORGANIZATION PROGRAM (PPO)?   YES   NO

[X] 15 DAY INITIAL   [ ] 45 DAY PROGRESS   SEE ITEM 1 ON REVERSE FOR FILING INSTRUCTIONS

[X] PHYSICIAN   [ ] PODIATRIST   [ ] CHIROPRACTOR

PLEASE TYPE ALL INFORMATION

STATE INSURANCE FUND

199 Church Street
New York, NY 10007

New York, NY

MD

In the circles are the standard codes to decsribe the treament. The \$94.69 etc is the cost.

Other Lesion Of Median Nerve
Sprain Of Unspecified Site Of Hand

812.00 Closed fx of pro humerus

Dates of Service To YY MM DD YY	Place of Service	Leave Blank	Procedures, Services or Supplies (Explain Unusual Circumstances) CPT/HCPCS	MODIFIER	Diagnosis Code	\$ Charges	Days or Units	COB	Zip Code Where Service was Rendered
	11		73030		1,2,3	94 69	1		10128
	11		73120		1,2	63 48	1		10128
	11		99024		1,2,3	0 00	1		10128

16. Patient's Account No. 337770

16. Total Charge 158 17

THE INJURED WORKER SHOULD NOT PAY THIS BILL

APPENDIX G
Mortality Table

This sample Mortality Table which issued by the Social Security Administration shows life expectancy by gender of Americans based on their current age. (Can be found at www.ssa.gov/oact/STATS/table4c6.html)

The purpose of this table being in this book is not to allow you to calculate your life expectancy but to help understand one of the many formulas carriers use when they make that calculation.

Note: The period life expectancy at a given age for 2007 represents the average number of years of life remaining if a group of persons at that age were to experience the mortality rates for 2007 over the course of their remaining life.

Age	Male	Female	Age	Male	Female	Age	Male	Female
21	55.47	60.23	41	36.93	40.97	61	20.16	23.14
22	54.54	59.26	42	36.02	40.03	62	19.40	22.31
23	53.63	58.29	43	35.12	39.10	63	18.66	21.49
24	52.71	57.32	44	34.22	38.17	64	17.92	20.69
25	51.78	56.35	45	33.33	37.24	65	17.19	19.89
26	50.86	55.38	46	32.45	36.32	66	16.48	19.10
27	49.93	54.40	47	31.57	35.41	67	15.77	18.32
28	49.00	53.44	48	30.71	34.50	68	15.08	17.55
29	48.07	52.47	49	29.84	33.59	69	14.40	16.79
30	47.13	51.50	50	28.99	32.69	70	13.73	16.05
31	46.20	50.53	51	28.15	31.80	71	13.08	15.32
32	45.27	49.56	52	27.32	30.91	72	12.44	14.61
33	44.33	48.60	53	26.49	30.02	73	11.82	13.91
34	43.40	47.64	54	25.68	29.14	74	11.21	13.22
35	42.47	46.68	55	24.87	28.27	75	10.62	12.55
36	41.54	45.72	56	24.06	27.40	76	10.04	11.90
37	40.61	44.76	57	23.26	26.53	77	9.48	11.26
38	39.68	43.81	58	22.48	25.67	78	8.94	10.63
39	38.76	42.86	59	21.69	24.82	79	8.41	10.03
40	37.84	41.91	60	20.92	23.97	80	7.90	9.43

This is taken from http://www.ssa.gov/oact/STATS/table4c6.html

There are also tables published by government agencies, hospitals, and research institutes. For example, there is the commonly referenced Morbidity Rate (survival rate) for various types of cancers. The tables, broken down by type of cancer, indicate the life expectancy by age.

Insurance companies use similar but far more detailed tables. Over the years there have been millions of not only work-related injuries but non-work related injuries that are the same as the work-related ones, Pulmonary diseases, heart conditions, bad backs, and thousands of other medical problems are take into account by carriers in estimating how much longer the injured worker will live. And, as the table below shows, as a person gets older their life expectancy changes.

While there are statistical tables shared by all the insurance industry, each carrier has developed their own tables to use as well, tables modified based on their own experience. The carrier whose tables and formulas are the most accurate, can make the best guess how much longer someone will live, like a bookie setting odds.

An injured worker will not be able to do these calculations because they do not have access to the same detailed tables as do the carriers. For example, the life expectancy table above will change dramatically if someone has a heart attack at age 60 or a bad back at age 40. In addition, the full table on the Social Security website has additional columns, including one showing how many people are left at each age bracket starting at 100,000 for the group of one-year old males. At Age 60, there are 85,227 males still living; at age 80, the male population is down to 47,974, i.e., those healthy enough to have made it that far have a longer life expectancy.

Essentially, as you get old, life expectancy increases, but only because all those who had major illness or accidents were deceased. One reason you can not use a table like this to calculate life expectancy is that, if you have a workers compensation claim for which a settlement is on the table, the odds are that whatever injury or illness you have has, statistically, had some negative effect on your life expectancy, even if only by two weeks.

CRITICAL CRITICAL

APPENDIX H
Annuity Agreements

One key issue that arises when annuity agreements are used in §32 agreement concerns the starting date of the payments, ending date of the payments, and what happens if the claimant dies before the entire amount is paid out.

There are two basic types of annuities: those which are fixed term and those which are lifetime, but may have a minimum payout period.

On occasion, the agreement calls for the annuity payment to begin not on the date of the approval of the agreement but to some prior date; this is usually when the annuity deal is completed and the rates are *'locked'* in by the insurer. As a result, there are a number of issues to be resolved depending on whether payments of the annuities have already started and/or if the claimant is getting a Continuing Compensation Payment (CCP).

1. FIXED TERM - NO CCP
   a. Did the annuity payments start already and, if yes, does the agreement reflect that fact. The issue of what happens if the agreement is not approved is not relevant with regards to the approval of same
   b. If the annuity payment did not start
     (i) Are retroactive payment to be made?
     (ii) Will the claimant waive his right to any possible late payment penalties that could be raised?
     (iii) Will the start date and, of course, the ending date be changed?

2. FIXED TERM - WITH CCP
   a. Did the annuity payments start already and, if yes, does the agreement reflect that fact?
     (i) What about overpayments?
     (ii) Is the carrier to date a credit or does this mean that nothing will change because, in effect, the annuity is really for a fixed sum to be paid out over time, so whether the installment started earlier or later is not relevant.

3. LIFE OF CLAIMANT - NO CCP

a. Did the annuity payments start already and, if yes, does the agreement reflect that fact?
   (i) Is there any impact on the agreement if these payment have already started or is the carrier accepting the '*cost*' of pre-approval payment?
   (ii) If not, how is it to be solved?

4.   LIFE OF CLAIMANT - WITH CCP
   a. Did the annuity payments start already and, if yes, does the agreement reflect that fact?
   b. If the annuity stared and the CCP continued, is the carrier waiving what may be an overpayment? If not, how is the overpayment to be done? Should be in the §32.
   c. If the annuity started and the CCP was stopped did the claimant and carrier have a written agreement to this effect, lest at some later date a demand is made of payment of the periods for which the CCP was stopped without formal WCB approval

There may be other issues with the annuity payment program which is usually an addendum to the §32 agreement and can run anywhere from one to ten pages.

These annuity agreements are another example of how the attorney or a licensed representative can play an important role in negotiating a §32 agreement.

CRITICAL

APPENDIX I

<u>NYCRR §300.36 Section 32 agreements</u>

Statement of purpose. To encourage the parties in interest to enter into agreements settling upon and determining the compensation and other benefits due to the claimant or the claimant's dependents.

a. The parties in interest to a claim for compensation may settle upon and determine any and all issues and matters by agreement, in accordance with section 32 of the Workers' Compensation Law, subject to the terms and conditions of this rule.

b. Any agreement submitted to the board for approval shall be on a form prescribed by the chair or, alternatively, contain the information prescribed by the chair.

c. The receipt of an agreement by the board for approval shall act as a stay on all related proceedings before the board.

d. An agreement submitted pursuant to section 32 of the Workers' Compensation Law shall not be binding on the parties in interest unless it is approved by the chair, a designee of the chair, a member of the board, or a Workers' Compensation Law Judge. The agreement shall be approved unless it is determined that:

1. the agreement is unfair, unconscionable, or improper as a matter of law; or

2. the agreement is the result of an intentional misrepresentation of a material fact; or

3. within 10 days of submission of the agreement, the board has received from any party in interest a written request that the agreement be disapproved by the board.

e. The agreement shall be reviewed by the chair, a designee of the chair, a member of the board, or a Workers' Compensation Law Judge, who will make a determination whether to approve or disapprove the agreement. The chair, designee of the chair, member of the board, or Workers' Compensation Law Judge reviewing the agreement may approve or disapprove the agreement administratively, based on a review of the record before the board, or may choose to schedule a meeting to question the parties about the agreement. If the agreement is reviewed administratively, the Board shall advise the parties in writing of the date the agreement shall be deemed submitted for the purposes of section 32 of the Workers' Compensation Law and this section. If a meeting is scheduled to question the parties about the agreement, the agreement will be deemed submitted for the purposes of Section 32 of the Workers' Compensation Law and this section at such meeting. No agreement shall be approved for a period of 10 calendar days after submission to the board.

f. The board will advise the parties of the approval or disapproval of all agreements by duly filing and serving a notice of approval or disapproval.

g.   An agreement which is approved shall be final and conclusive on the parties in interest, and shall not be subject to review pursuant to section 23 of the Workers' Compensation Law. An agreement which is disapproved shall be subject to review pursuant to section 23 of the Workers' Compensation Law.

h. The carrier shall make payments of any award as required in the agreement within 10 days of the filing of the decision approving the agreement. If the carrier fails to make such payments, the carrier shall be subject to penalties pursuant to paragraph (f) of subdivision 3 of section 25 of the Workers' Compensation Law.

i. An agreement may provide for reasonable fees commensurate with the services rendered by the claimant's attorney or licensed representative. Whenever a fee is requested in excess of $ 450, the requested fee is to be made upon form OC-400.1 attached to the submitted agreement.

j Any agreement submitted and approved pursuant to section 32 of the Workers' Compensation Law and this rule may be modified at anytime by agreement of all parties in interest provided such modification is approved by the board.

CR80CR80CR80CR80

APPENDIX J

<u>Closed means 'CLOSED'</u>

For those claimants who feel that they have a problem with their settlement that warrants a reopening and that their case is the exception to the rule, the Courts of the State of New York have made it quite clear that the Board may not review the terms of a Section 32 Settlement Agreement once it has been approved.

WCL §32(c) states:

> A decision duly filed and served approving an agreement submitted to the board shall not be subject to review pursuant to section twenty-three of this article.

Among the many cases supporting WCL §32(c), including one just issued, are

> Cooper v Cosmopolitan Care decided by the New York State Appellate court, Third Department on November 13, 2011.

> the *Matter of Estate of Lutz v. Lakeside Beaker Nursing Home*, 301 AD2d 688, 753 NYS2d 190, leave dismissed 99 NY2d 651, 760 NYS2d 104 (3rd Dept. 2003)

And

> the *Matter of Drummond v. The Desmond*, 295 AD2d 711, 744 NYS2d 224, leave denied 98 NY2d 615, 752 NYS2d 1 (3rd Dept. 2002).

In the *Matter of Drummond*, the New York State Appellate Court, Third Department, specifically opined the following:

> The right to apply for both administrative and appellate review pursuant to Workers' Compensation Law §23 is expressly limited when, as here, a claimant (or a deceased claimant's dependents) and the employer or its workers' compensation carrier enter into a waiver agreement and that agreement is approved by the Board.

Under such circumstances, Workers' Compensation Law §32 explicitly provides that "*[a] decision duly filed and served approving an agreement submitted to the board shall not be subject to review pursuant to [WCL §23]*" (WCL §32 [c] [emphasis supplied]; see, 12 NYCRR §300.36 [f]). Accordingly, neither the Board nor this Court may review a waiver agreement once it has been approved.

The very limited circumstances under which the Board can review an approved 32 agreement are:

(1) If it was clearly issued in error;
(2) To determine whether a specific condition was included in the settlement;
(3) To examine the issue of late-payment penalty, per 12 NYCRR §300.36(g);

or

(4) To determine proper allocation of attorney's fees per WCL §24.

The purpose of the §32 settlement, a defined in §32(c) and supported by the Court, is to close the case forever.

CROCROCROCRO

APPENDIX K

MEDICARE SET ASIDE DISCLOSURE FORM

I, _____, have been advised by my attorney, _____, that

- The Medicare Secondary Payor regulations say Medicare is always secondary to workers' comp and other insurance, including no-fault and liability insurance. Under the Social Security Act, payment *"may not be made under Medicare for covered items or services to the extent that payment has been made, or can reasonably be expected to be made promptly, under a liability insurance policy or plan."*

- Medicare will not pay for any medical expenses related to the injury after settlement until any portion of the settlement/judgment that is allocated to future medical expenses covered by Medicare has been fully exhausted.

- If any portion of the settlement/judgment has been allocated to future medical expenses, some portion of the settlement/judgment may need to be set aside into an account as an adequate representation of Medicare's interest in my future cost of care.

- A Medicare set-aside ('*MSA*') allocation amount is determined through the detailed analysis of each particular case. Once this '*set aside*' amount is exhausted, Medicare becomes the primary payor of Medicare covered expenses for those settlement-related injuries or judgment-related injuries.

- Further protection is available if I were to obtain approval from the Centers for Medicare and Medicaid Services ('*CMS*') of the proposed MSA value. Only when these funds have been exhausted will I be able to utilize my Medicare card for future injury-related services or expenses.

- Although CMS approval of the MSA calculation is not mandatory, it helps avoid problems with future Medicare coverage. It also ensures that only a predefined portion of my settlement/judgment, rather than the entire settlement/judgment, must be spent before Medicare takes over payment again. I understand that seeking and receiving CMS approval of the set aside amount is the only way to guarantee that

Medicare's future interests and my future Medicare benefits have been fully protected.

- MSA proceeds must be used only for *injury-specific medical expenses*, which Medicare would have paid. Compliance with all Medicare rules and regulations is mandatory, including showing Medicare that money in the MSA account was spent properly. I can opt to either self-administer my own set-aside funds or may purchase a plan through an MSA administration company to ensure that my funds are properly spent and disbursed. If I choose to self-administer the funds, it is my obligation to ensure that the MSA funds are used properly. Improper administration of the funds could result in the loss of my Medicare eligibility.

- If an MSA is required, I, or my custodian, must keep and submit, upon request or at year-end to CMS, all of the medical bills and receipts associated with the payment of injury-related, Medicare-approved medical expenses.

- MSA proceeds only may be used to pay for pharmaceuticals upon the condition that the MSA proposal accounted for such expenses; otherwise no MSA proceeds may be used for the purchase of medication.

_____   _____

CLIENT   DATE

STATE OF _____, COUNTY OF

_____

Subscribed, sworn to and acknowledged before me by

_____, the Client, this ____day of _____,
2011.

NOTARY PUBLIC
My Commission Expires: _____

Cฆฆฆฆฆฆฆฆฆ

GLOSSARY

Allocation Rate: Since Social Security looks at other forms of income, including workers' compensation awards, if the claimant receives an advance payment (lump sum or §32 settlement), a calculation must be made to determine what would be the weekly value of the lump sum settlement; the result is called an *'allocation rate'*. The *'allocation'* rate is inserted in the §32 agreement and is almost always in Lump Sum Agreements if there is any possibility that the claimant may be in the process of getting Social Security or Social Security Disability or may already be collecting it. This is a weekly rate and is usually the same as the amount of the compensation award the claimant has been receiving

Appliances refers, in workers' compensation terms, to crutches, prosthetic limbs, eyeglasses, wheelchairs, TENS units, special beds, Whirlpool baths, specially equipped motor vehicles, false teeth, etc.

Carrier: used instead of *'insurance company'* probably because it is shorter.

Classification: A determination by a law judge to the effect that the claimant's condition is both stable and has been measured as meeting one of the classifications of disability: mild, moderate, total, etc. The medical status is sometimes referred to as MMI: Maximum Medical Improvement, meaning that additional treatment or therapy will not improve the medical status/level of disability of the injured worker.

'Closed' Case in workers' compensation law means that there are no pending issues being fought over, hence the file could be closed for now. Until the advent of the §32, a case/claim could never be closed, i.e put in a file cabinet never to be opened again on any issue pertaining to that case/claim. Now that there are §32's, the term *'closed'* can either mean (1) closed permanently, forever as is the purpose of a §32 or (2) closed in that the case has, at the time it is closed, has no open issues but is a case which can be reopened again if the injured workers' condition changes.

Sometime the Board uses the term *'NFA'*. This mean *'No Further Action'* and better represents a *'closed'* case which is not *'closed'* in the §32 sense but in the sense that it has become *'inactive.'*

CMS: Centers for Medicare & Medicaid Services (CMS) is the entity created by the Federal government to insure that the interests of Medicare are protected. With regards to workers' compensation, CMS has an interest in the Medicare Set-Aside.

Disability (Partial): Disability which allows a claimant to engage in some kind of gainful employment. The difference between the claimant's pre-accident earnings and post-accident earnings is determinative of the reduced earnings rate. (WC law § 15, Sub.5, 5-a)

Disability (Total): Disability which precludes a claimant from earning any wages. (WC law § 15, Sub.1,2)

Interested Parties: anyone who has an interest in what happens with the agreement but has no legal rights to participate in the settlement. See Chapter 12 - *Who Participates in the agreement*, page 92.

Lump Sum Settlement: the form of settlement agreement in effect before §32's. Settled only the awards but not medical treatment. See Chapter 2 - *Settlements prior to §32's*, page 12.

Maximum Medical Improvement (MMI): a term that is used when it is determined by the doctors (or a law judge if the doctors disagree) that the claimant has reached the maximum level of improvement that he can and that additional treatment or therapy will not improve the medical status/level of disability of the injured worker. A finding of maximum medical improvement is a normal precondition for determining the permanent disability level of a claimant.

Medicare Set Aside (MSA) is a sum of money allocated from a settlement which presents the expected future medical costs that are to be paid for by the claimant. This set aside is done to prevent the shifting of responsibility for paying fr medical expenses from a primary payer to the Medicare program. MSAs have become standard practice in many workers' compensation claims and in some liability claims based on Medicare directives. See Chapter 13 - *Medicare & Set-Asides*, page 98.

NYCRR - New York Codes, Rules, and Regulations is the name for a section of the law written usually written by each agency/board which goes into detail as to how that agency conducts its day-to-day activities.

Occupational Disease (OD) A disease arising from employment conditions for a class of worker, with the disease occurring as a natural incident for particular occupations, distinct from and exceeding the ordinary hazards and risks of employment. To be considered an occupational disease, there must be some recognizable link between the disease and some distinctive features of the worker's job. (WC law § 2 (15), 3(2), 37)

Parties of interest: the only ones who can sign the agreement. See Chapter 12 - *Who Participates in the agreement*, page 92.

Second Injury Fund: Unofficial name for the Special Disability Fund established to encourage employers to hire workers with physical handicaps. When workers with pre-existing conditions suffer further work-related injuries, or disease, that results in a greater disability, the employer, through the insurer, is responsible for only part of the benefits. The Second Injury Fund is responsible for the rest (WC law § 15, Sub. 8). This provision no longer applies for loss dates after June 30, 2007. See Chapter 12 - *Who Participates in the Agreement*, page 92.

Special Funds: The Special Funds Conservation Committee (the '*Special Funds*') was organized in 1938 for the purpose of conserving assets of the special funds, created under Subdivision 8 of §15 and §25-a of the WCL of the State of New York.

The Executive Committee of the Special Funds consists of five voting members, one each to represent the stock carriers, the mutual carriers, the State Insurance Fund, the New York Compensation Insurance Rating Board and self-insurers. There are also three non-voting advisory members representing the American Insurance Association, the New York State Insurance Association and the Alliance of American Insurers.

INDEX

CRUCRUCRUCRU

Behind The Closed Doors

An insider's look at how things really work at the NYS Workers Compensation Board -And how to fix them.

Behind The Closed Doors

An insider's look at how things *really* work at the NYS Workers' Compensation Board and how to fix them!

Michael T. Berns
NYS Workers' Compensation Commissioner
1996-2008

Created in 1914, the NYS Workers' Compensation Board has attempted to keep up with changes in the labor market and technology, most notably a computer system being used to manage a system that annually handles more than 250,000 injuries and nearly $6 billions in awards for lost wages and medical expenses. That the system work as well as it does is a credit to the 1,500 civil servants and political appointees who work there. But there is a great deal more than can be done, and should be done. The system should be more responsive to the needs of the injured workers, as well as those employers whose insurance premiums not only pay workers' lost wages and medical expenses, but also pay all the expenses of running the Board. Having served nearly 12 years on the Board, trying to fix the system from the inside, under three governors and four chairman, former Commissioner Mike Berns tells the real story of how the system works - and what can be done to make it better.

©2008 $19.95   www.createspace.com/3358424

TABLE OF CONTENTS

154

CR∞CR∞CR∞CR∞

ABOUT THE AUTHOR

Michael Berns was nominated to the New York State Workers' Compensation Board by Governor George E. Pataki and confirmed by the State Senate in 1996, and in again in 2000 and 2006, serving as a Commissioner until 2008. The author of several key legal decisions affirmed by The Court of Appeals, the state's highest court, Berns annually participated in approximately 5,000 workers' compensations claims decisions. He was also active in developing methods to enhance the consistency of these decisions, as well as helping in the Board's conversion from a paper-based adjudication and claims system into a more modern computer based system.

In November 2008, Berns published a book about the Board, its philosophy, policies, and practices:

> _Behind The Closed Doors - An insider's look at how things really work at the NYS Workers Compensation Board -And how to fix them._

In addition, since November 2008, Berns has been the editor and publisher of the website www.InsideWorkersCompNY.com. This website, published weekly, analyzes the New York State Appellate Court's and Court of Appeal's reviews of Board decisions as well as suppling up-to-date news on issues of interest to the workers' compensation community in New York.

In addition, commentaries on workers' compensation related issues and various statistical reports are published weekly along with submissions from guest writers, including lawyers and medical professional serving the community.

Prior to his being appointed to the Board, Berns served as the chief executive of several firms involved in the international distribution of American manufactured products for which he was primarily responsible for establishing distribution and manufacturing facilities throughout the world. Berns has also served as an officer of, or on the board of, companies ranging from real estate to manufacturing, and as a director of a number community based organizations, including serving as a member of Manhattan's Community Board 8.

A member of the cast of Lincoln Center's Metropolitan Opera for 18 seasons, Berns has also published articles on real estate and computer programming.

Berns graduated from the Wharton School at the University of Pennsylvania with a Bachelor of Science in Economics, and completed additional studies as an undergraduate at the Universidad Nacional de Mexico in Mexico City and New York University as well as graduate studies at New York University's Stern School of Business. He currently lives in New York City with his wife and family.